Comanche Peak WILDERNESS AREA

HIKING & SNOWSHOEING GUIDE

Joe and Frédérique Grim

The Colorado Mountain Club Press
Golden, Colorado

Comanche Peak Wilderness Area Hiking and Snowshoeing Guide
© 2010 Joe and Frédérique Grim

All rights reserved. No part of this publication may be reproduced or transmitted in any form or by any means, electronic or mechanical, including photocopy, recording, or by any information storage and retrieval system without permission in writing from the publisher.

PUBLISHED BY

The Colorado Mountain Club Press
710 Tenth Street, Suite 200, Golden, Colorado 80401
303-996-2743   e-mail: cmcpress@cmc.org

Founded in 1912, The Colorado Mountain Club is the largest outdoor recreation, education, and conservation organization in the Rocky Mountains. Look for our books at your local bookstore or outdoor retailer or online at www.cmc.org/books.

Alan Bernhard: design, composition, and production
Alan Stark: publisher

CONTACTING THE PUBLISHER
We would appreciate it if readers would alert us to any errors or outdated information by contacting us at the address above.

DISTRIBUTED TO THE BOOK TRADE BY
Mountaineers Books, 1001 SW Klickitat Way, Suite 201, Seattle, WA
98134, 800-553-4453, www.mountaineersbooks.org

COVER PHOTO: Looking toward the Emmaline Lake cirque from the route to Comanche Peak.

We gratefully acknowledge the financial support of the people of Colorado through the Scientific and Cultural Facilities District of greater metropolitan Denver for our publishing activities.

The base art for the maps in this book are used courtesy of the USGS.

WARNING: Although there has been an effort to make the trail descriptions in this book as accurate as possible, some discrepancies may exist between the text and the trails in the field. Hiking in mountainous areas is a high-risk activity. This guidebook is not a substitute for your experience and common sense. The users of this guidebook assume full responsibility for their own safety. Weather, terrain conditions, and individual abilities must be considered before undertaking any of the hikes in this guide.

First Edition
ISBN 978-0-9842213-1-8

Printed in China

CONTENTS

CROWN POINT SECTION

UPPER POUDRE SECTION

ACKNOWLEDGMENTS

First, we would like to thank those who have made the Comanche Peak Wilderness possible: the US Forest Service, those who originally sought to protect this impressive Wilderness, and those who volunteer to maintain these wonderful trails. For their review of this book, we would like to thank Jim Shaklee, Steve Martin, Terri Gerard, Paul Weber, and John Paul Lumpp. We would also like to acknowledge those who joined us on many of these hikes, including, but not limited to: Terri Gerard, Steve Martin, Manuel Fillon, Mary Jackson, and Paul Weber. And finally, we would like to thank our families for encouraging us to write this book.

Queen's Crown is one of many types of flowers that can be found along the Brackenbury Cabin Trail.

PREFACE

Since first stepping into this area, we knew this place was special. From its flower-filled meadows to its burbling brooks to its alpine tundra to its towering peaks, the Comanche Peak Wilderness is a unique and beautiful area. Often overlooked in favor of neighboring Rocky Mountain National Park, it doesn't see that many visitors, yet it's only an hour from Fort Collins. Since moving to Colorado in 2005, we have taken every chance we've had to get out into the mountains. We have always appreciated the beauty of God's creation, but at first we were unaware that we were sometimes leaving behind avoidable traces of our presence. We have since joined several groups (The Colorado Mountain Club, Poudre Wilderness Volunteers, and Cameron Pass Nordic Rangers) whose goals include getting people out into the mountains, and, more importantly, educating them about how to be good stewards of the wilderness. As a result, although this book serves as a comprehensive guidebook to the Comanche Peak Wilderness, our greater hope is that it will help us all to enjoy this beautiful area and to leave it pristine for generations to come.

Alpine Sunflowers seen near the summit of Crown Point.

OVERVIEW OF THE COMANCHE PEAK WILDERNESS

With the *Wilderness Act of 1964*, Congress first officially designated nearly nine million acres of our national lands as protected wilderness, providing specific regulations that have helped ensure that each of these areas would be "an area where the earth and its community of life are untrammeled by man, where man himself is a visitor who does not remain . . . an area protected and managed so as to preserve its natural conditions." In 1980, Congress added the Comanche Peak Wilderness to its list of protected wilderness areas; since that time, the National Wilderness Preservation System has come to encompass 109 million acres.

The Comanche Peak Wilderness is named for its prominent 12,709-foot peak that lies along its southern boundary with Rocky Mountain National Park. Unlike the National Park, this area receives relatively few visitors. However, the rustic beauty of the Comanche Peak Wilderness is comparable to (and we would argue even better than) Rocky Mountain National Park.

The Canyon Lakes District of the Arapaho and Roosevelt National Forests officially maintains nineteen trails within the Comanche Peak Wilderness, all of which are described in this book. Destinations along or near these trails include eight lakes, sixteen named rivers and creeks, and two named waterfalls. In addition to its namesake, the Comanche Peak Wilderness has six other named peaks and numerous other unnamed, but equally impressive, peaks. Route descriptions to each of the named peaks, as well as a few other interesting off-trail destinations, are included alongside the trail descriptions.

It should be kept in mind that although we have made every effort to make this information as accurate as possible, we can make no guarantee that this guidebook is perfect. Trail rules and regulations may change with time, so please make sure that you check with the United States Forest Service (USFS) for all up-to-date rules and regulations (www.fs.fed.us/r2/arnf/recreation/trails/clrd).

Sheep Creek Meadow provides great wetland habitat for waterfowl and fish.

It is also a very good idea to read all trailhead signs, as different trails often have different regulations. A common example is whether or not and when horses may be ridden on the trail. Stiff fines can result from improper use of a trail.

Since the Canyon Lakes District borders on Rocky Mountain National Park, several of the trails cross into the Park. This guidebook's descriptions of these National Forest trails end at the first major feature within the National Park. There are numerous Rocky Mountain National Park trail guides in which you can find descriptions of the remaining portions of these trails.

The trails in the Comanche Peak Wilderness are most easily hiked in the summer, when the paths are free of snow and ice; however, six of the fourteen trailheads are open year-round, and a couple of other trailheads can be accessed with just a short hike (or snowshoe) up a Forest Service road, allowing you to experience this wonderful Wilderness any time of the year. If snowshoeing any of the trails up Pingree Park Road, keep in mind that this road can sometimes be quite treacherous in the winter. Several of the Forest Development Roads (FDRs) do not open until June or early July, and fall snowstorms may close roads earlier than anticipated, so check the USFS Web site at www.fs.fed.us/r2/arnf/conditions/forest-roads/clrd/index.shtml for the latest information on road closures.

Eight of the nineteen trails have designated campsites along the way, making this area a wonderful place for backcountry camping. Be aware, however, that most of the campsites are in USFS Travel Zones, where campfires are prohibited, so don't forget to bring your camp stove.

Additional photos, descriptions, maps, and information about the trails and hikes in the Comanche Peak Wilderness are available at **www.joeandfrede.com/comanche.htm**.

KEEPING OUR WILDERNESS WILD
Leave No Trace

All of us who love the pristine beauty of the wilderness want it to retain its untouched appearance forever. However, the only way we can really enjoy its beauty is to be surrounded by the mountains, lakes, forests, and streams. Therefore it is important that we reduce our impact as much as possible, so that we *Leave No Trace* of our presence for others, who will later walk where we have.

The practice of Leave No Trace typically follows seven principles: 1) Plan ahead and prepare; 2) Travel and camp on durable surfaces; 3) Dispose of waste properly; 4) Leave what you find; 5) Minimize campfire impacts; 6) Respect wildlife; and 7) Be considerate of other visitors. Each principle is important, and it only takes a small amount of effort and preparation to follow these principles.

Plan ahead and prepare.

- Of course, it's important to plan ahead and prepare for any dangers that you might encounter, but it's also very important to be prepared and have the proper knowledge to minimize your impact on nature. This includes:
  — Knowing the regulations for the area you'll visit (for more on this, see the following section)
  — Choosing equipment and supplies that will help you Leave No Trace

Travel and camp on durable surfaces.

- We must admit, we like to get off the beaten path and see places very few others get to, but we also realize that it is important to use preexisting paths whenever possible. If your hike does take you off-trail, it is important to try your best to travel on durable surfaces, namely, rock, gravel, dry grasses, and snow.

- If your group consists of a few people or more and you are not on a maintained trail, it is also important to spread out a little so that you are not creating a trodden path. This is particularly important in fragile alpine areas and wetlands.
- The key to campsites is that the best ones are found, not made. In the time it would take you to make your own site, you likely would be able to find a suitable site where your impacts would be minimized. It is also a good idea to use preexisting sites and sites that are out of view of the trail and other people.

Dispose of waste properly.

- Put simply, if you pack it in, you should pack it out.
- Part of principle 1 (plan ahead and prepare) is to repackage your food and supplies before heading out so that you minimize the waste you have to carry out.
- Deposit human waste in holes that are 6–8 inches deep.

Leave what you find.

- If you take something out of the wilderness, no one else will ever be able to see that item in its natural environment. Even if it's only something little, remember that if everyone took a little bit, it might make a big difference in the end. Instead of taking something out of the wilderness, photograph it.

Minimize campfire impacts.

- Use camp stoves and/or keep campfires small. Campfires literally bake the ground beneath them, making it difficult for plants to regrow at that location.
- Create small fire rings to contain fires, both for safety and to minimize their impact.
- If you make a campfire ring, destroy it when you're done, and scatter the *cold* ashes, so that no one can tell you had a campfire there.

The North Fork Trail passes by several beaver dams on the North Fork of the Big Thompson River.

- Only use dead wood for campfires. In addition to the fact that using green wood requires damaging live trees, it also doesn't burn very well.

Respect wildlife.

- Help keep wildlife wild. Don't approach wild creatures, feed them, or leave out food that they can get into.
- Be sure to maintain control of your pets. In designated Wilderness, pets must be on a handheld leash at all times.

Be considerate of other visitors.

- Be courteous.
- Try to keep your noise level down so that others can enjoy the sounds of nature.
- By following the first six principles, you are also following the seventh principle by providing a pristine setting for others to enjoy.

For more information on Leave No Trace principles, visit the Leave No Trace Center for Outdoor Ethics at www.lnt.org or the local USFS volunteer organization at www.poudrewildernessvolunteers.org.

EXPERIENCING AND ENJOYING OUR WILDERNESS

Wilderness Rules and Regulations

The rules and regulations for our wilderness areas are not there to make things harder on us or to restrict our fun; rather they were made so that we, and generations to come, can all experience and enjoy the pristine nature of our wilderness.

Current rules and regulations for the Comanche Peak Wilderness include:

- Camping and fire building are prohibited within 200 feet of all lakes, streams, and trails to protect water quality, sensitive vegetation, and access by animals, and to help assure solitude.
- Groups entering or spending time in the Wilderness for day or overnight use are restricted to a combined maximum of twelve people and livestock. No permit is required.
- Dogs must be kept on a handheld leash in the Comanche Peak Wilderness. There is a fine for not keeping your dog on a leash. Unleashed dogs can harass wildlife, can create conflicts between visitors, and can become lost or injured.

A poisonous Fly Amanita found along the Big South Trail.

- Recreational pack stock must not be hobbled, tethered, or picketed within 200 feet of any lakes, streams, or trails. This protects fragile vegetation and keeps lakes and streams clean. To avoid damage to the trunks and roots of trees and to help preserve the area's wilderness character, tethering or tying livestock to live trees is prohibited. Use of a highline or picket line is acceptable.
- Certified weed-free forage is required on all public lands. This feed should also be fed to stock starting 48 to 72 hours prior to entering public lands, so that they do not carry weed seeds onto public lands.
- Travel methods are restricted to foot or horseback. Neither motorized nor mechanized equipment, vehicles, or machines are allowed in wilderness areas. Mountain bikes and other wheeled conveyances are not permitted in the Wilderness. Some of these trails start a significant distance outside of the designated Wilderness; for these trails, bikes are typically allowed up to the Wilderness boundary, although it is also important to check the sign at the trailhead, as exceptions do exist.
- Many Comanche Peak Wilderness trails cross into Rocky Mountain National Park; be sure to note rule changes when you cross into the Park. The most notable rule change is that dogs are not allowed on any trail in the Park.
- Volunteer wilderness rangers patrol the area and will inform visitors, as needed, of regulations and low-impact techniques for camping.
- Practice Leave No Trace principles.

There are five areas within the Comanche Peak Wilderness that have been designated as Travel Zones by the US Forest Service, giving them an extra level of protection. These Travel Zones are: Browns Lake, Comanche Lake, Emmaline, Big South Fork (of the Cache la Poudre River), and the North Fork (of the

A section of the North Boundary Trail passes over a soft bed of lodgepole pine needles.

Big Thompson River). In these areas the following additional rules apply:

- Camping is restricted to designated campsites. USFS Travel Zones are marked along their trails and also at their trailheads; the National Geographic Trails Illustrated maps also provide a very good depiction of their boundaries.

- No more than twelve people with three tents can use one campsite. Tents must be within 30 feet of the campsite marker. Do not camp or build a fire in revegetative sites. These areas are seeded with native, high-altitude grasses and need protection to grow.

- Campfires are prohibited in the Travel Zones. Campfires consume scarce vegetation and leave permanent scars on the fragile soils of the area. Please use a backcountry stove. Wood fires are only allowed outside the designated Travel Zones.

- Stock animals are prohibited from remaining overnight within all Travel Zones. In addition, stock animals are prohibited at all times within the Emmaline Travel Zone.

HAVING A GOOD *AND SAFE* HIKE

It is important to always be prepared for the worst when hiking in the wild. Even though most trips do not end up requiring the use of a lot of equipment, difficult situations can and do arise that require the use of extra equipment. If your life ends up depending on it one day, you'll be glad you were prepared.

Be sure to bring the so-called "ten essentials," which include (but aren't limited to):

- map
    — maps included in this manual are for illustration purposes only; it is best to use 1:24000-scale 7.5-minute USGS topographic maps or National Geographic Trails Illustrated maps.
- compass and/or GPS (we suggest both, so you have a backup)
- sunscreen
- pocket knife
- flashlight/headlamp
- extra batteries
- extra food and water
- extra layers of clothes
- first aid kit
- fire starter kit

In addition, it is often helpful to have:
- water treatment device/chemicals
- trekking poles or walking stick
- bug repellent
- repair kit (for your pack and/or tent)
- signaling devices
- tarp or bivy sack for emergency shelter

Where the trail is faint, tree blazes often mark the way.

A sweeping view of the Never Summer and Medicine Bow Ranges, seen from the intersection of the Flowers and Mirror Lake Trails.

Also, it is important to think of any hike-specific items you might need. For travel on steep snow and ice-covered terrain, supplementary traction add-ons or snowshoes, an ice axe, pack shovel, and an avalanche beacon are important tools to bring along. If you plan on doing any scrambling, it is a good idea to bring along climbing equipment in case you inadvertently get yourself into a predicament.

It may seem like a pain to carry so much equipment, but difficult situations can arise, and it is best to be prepared in the unlikely event of an emergency. If you are many miles from the nearest road and you sprain an ankle, it could take a day or more to get to safety. Having an extra liter of water could make the difference between life and death. Having enough extra clothing and weather protection to keep you warm and dry through the night could save you from hypothermia. Even if the weather forecast is not calling for potentially hazardous weather, always be prepared for it anyway. As a meteorologist myself, I (Joe) can say that there is no such thing as no chance of precipitation. In most mountainous areas, it can potentially snow any time of the year. Just because it's warm, calm, and sunny now doesn't mean it won't be cold, windy, and rainy/snowy just an hour from now.

It is always important to have a detailed map with you, as well as a compass. Even if you have a GPS, a compass and map are things you can always fall back on if your GPS fails. Maps and compasses don't need batteries. It is also important to *fully know* how to use the navigation equipment you have, particularly if you go off the trail, but even if you stay on the trail. The remote sections of some trails are faint to practically nonexistent, so a detailed map and navigation device are needed to follow these

sections of trail. Many of the trails are marked by tree blazes in the forest and by rock cairns in alpine areas and meadows; it is always good to keep an eye out for these. When there is snow on the trail (there can be at least patchy snow during all but a couple months each year), it can be particularly difficult to follow the trail. We hike many of these trails year-round, but in order to write this book, we had to hike most of the trails in the summer at least once to make sure our GPS waypoints were actually on the trails. Other signs you can use to determine that you are on the trail when there is deep snow are cut logs. Volunteers give up their time in the summer to clear the trails of downfall, and as a result you typically see quite a bit of cut downfall along the trails. If it has been a while since you've seen a blaze or cut downfall, you might be off-trail, and should consider backtracking to the last place you saw one. Wind and falling snow can often fill in snowshoe tracks quickly, so don't rely on them to lead you back.

The most important thing to bring other than extra food and water is a first aid kit. You may never have a life-threatening injury on a hike, but if you do, having a first aid kit could save your life. It is also a good idea to not hike alone. If you are injured and cannot walk, your hiking partner will be able to go get help. The risk of an animal attack, though very rare, increases dramatically for a single hiker compared to two or more people hiking together. It is particularly important to keep small children close by at all times, as they are the most susceptible to animal attacks. If you would like to find people to hike with, there are numerous hiking groups in the area that regularly schedule outings, including The Colorado Mountain Club and the Poudre Wilderness Volunteers.

COMANCHE PEAK WILDERNESS OVERVIEW MAP

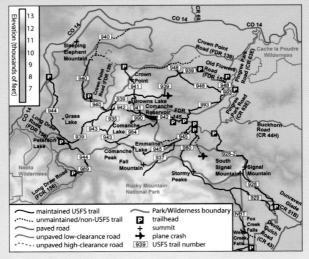

* Although this map is to scale, it is not intended for navigational purposes for your hike. We suggest you use the following National Geographic Trails Illustrated maps: Poudre River/Cameron Pass (#112), Cache La Poudre/Big Thompson (#101), and Rocky Mountain National Park (#200).

NOTE: CO = Colorado Route   CR = County Road
       FDR = Forest Development Road

KEY FOR TRAIL MAPS THROUGHOUT THE BOOK

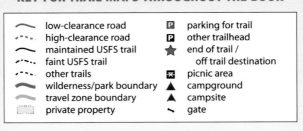

HOW TO USE THIS GUIDEBOOK

- Trail length and hike length distances are one-way unless otherwise noted. The distances listed for nearby destinations are one-way distances from the beginning of the hike.

- Waypoint mileages are cumulative. For example, on the North Fork Trail, the bridge #1 waypoint is at mile 0.8 on the hike, not 0.8 mile from the previous waypoint.

- Elevation listings represent the total elevation gain for one-way travel along the trail, the total elevation loss for one-way travel along the trail, and the altitude range (above sea level) of the trail.

- The difficulty rating is based on the overall difficulty of the trail, taking into consideration steepness, footing, and length.

- The stock rating is based on the difficulty level for stock and their riders. Additional stock regulations are also included.

- Maps are for illustrative purposes only; hikers should always take with them a detailed Trails Illustrated or USGS quad map. Detailed maps can be found at many hiking and book stores, as well as numerous places online, including the Web site for this guidebook: **www.joeandfrede.com/comanche.htm**.

- Season: Based on our firsthand experiences on many of these trails, we are providing our best estimates concerning when trailheads will be open, and when snowshoes will be necessary on the trail. However, trail conditions vary widely from one year to the next. Just because the trail is not usually snow-covered in September, does not mean it will not be snow-covered on the particular September day you decide to hike it.

North Fork Trail (#929)

TRAIL LENGTH	5.3 miles
ELEVATION GAIN, LOSS, RANGE	1,803 feet, 305 feet, 7,636–9,278 feet
DIFFICULTY RATING	Moderate; 8 percent average grade
STOCK RATING	Difficult
DOGS	Permitted on handheld leash within Wilderness up to National Park boundary
SEASON	Trailhead open year-round; snowshoes typically necessary December–March
TRAILS ILLUSTRATED MAPS	Cache La Poudre/Big Thompson (#101) and Rocky Mountain National Park (#200)
USGS 7.5-MINUTE QUADS	Estes Park and Glen Haven

COMMENT: This is a great trail in any season if you like pleasant hikes by streams and through the forest, as it follows the North Fork of the Big Thompson River, which provides lush habitat for wildlife and good fishing opportunities. Along the way it passes through several small meadows and near the remains of a pioneer homestead, each of which make a nice resting spot or final destination for your hike.

GETTING THERE: From Loveland, take US 34 west for 17 miles to Drake. Turn right on Devils Gulch Road (County Road 43) and travel 6.1 miles to Dunraven Glade Road (County Road 51B). Turn right and go 2.2 miles to the Dunraven Trailhead parking lot at the end of the public road.

TRAIL DESCRIPTION: The trail starts out by climbing up and over a small ridge to the south, where it enters the Comanche Peak Wilderness and the North Fork of the Big Thompson River valley. From here on, the trail stays in this beautiful valley. Initially, the trail winds its way through a narrow canyon in

One of many lush flower-filled meadows along the North Fork Trail.

somewhat open forest, although the forest becomes denser as the valley widens. Near the third bridge crossing, the trail enters the private property of Cheley Camp and passes by its many camp facilities. It is imperative that hikers stay on the trail through this area. Shortly before leaving the property, the trail crosses another bridge and follows the remnants of an old road. Just before crossing the fifth bridge, you will encounter the first of nine spur trails leading to National Forest designated campsites. These campsites are simple, with only a post marking their location, and they are on a first-come, first-served basis; however, there are enough that they rarely all fill up. Keep in mind that since this is in a USFS Travel Zone, you may camp only in these designated sites, and also must use camp stoves instead of campfires. The next stretch of trail passes through

Near the end of the Kettle Tarn campsite trail lies this little pool and a view of Mount Dickinson to the west.

dense, lush forest, as it is located on the south side of the valley, which receives much less sunshine. After crossing the sixth bridge to the north side of the creek, the trail enters into the first of several meadows. Meadows are more common on the north side of the creek, as it receives more sunlight and is therefore drier. At the far end of the meadow are the remnants of an old cabin. The trail then passes for 0.7 mile through alternating evergreen forest, meadows, and a few aspen stands, as it begins to climb a little more steeply. Starting at a switchback, the trail climbs a bit above the creek and enters into denser forest, interrupted only by one rocky overlook, which provides a nice view of Mount Dickinson to the west. The trail enters Rocky Mountain National Park at the 4.4 mile mark (this is where dogs and their owners must turn around), and continues through the forest for another 0.9 mile to its intersection with the North Boundary Trail. There are two short trails to reservable backcountry campsites along this stretch. It is worth taking the short hike toward the Kettle Tarn campsite, in order to see its namesake, Kettle Tarn: a small, quaint intermittent pond in a little depression. This campsite area is closed from late spring to early summer, so contact the National Park backcountry office at 970-586-1242 to see if it is open. This guidebook's description of the North Fork Trail ends at its intersection with the North Boundary Trail; however, the North Fork Trail continues in the National Park for another 4 miles to Lost Lake.

NORTH FORK TRAIL		
MILEAGE	**DESTINATIONS**	**GPS WAYPOINTS**
	Dunraven Trailhead	N40.4756 W105.4605
0.1	Enter Comanche Peak Wilderness	N40.4739 W105.4600
0.4	Intersection with unnamed trail leading to North Fork Road (turn right)	N40.4729 W105.4636
0.8	Bridge #1	N40.4730 W105.4704
0.9	Bridge #2	N40.4737 W105.4712
1.2	Intersection with trail leading to Cheley Camp	N40.4780 W105.4707
1.2	Bridge #3	N40.4781 W105.4709
1.2	Leave Wilderness and enter Cheley Camp property	N40.4785 W105.4712
1.5	Bridge #4	N40.4812 W105.4744
1.5	Road to Cheley Camp	N40.4816 W105.4745
1.6	Leave Cheley Camp property and reenter Wilderness	N40.4826 W105.4768
2.1	Trail to Campsite #1; Bridge #5	N40.4846 W105.4851
2.7	Trail to Campsite #2; Bridge #6; Trail to Campsite #3	N40.4876 W105.4949
2.8	Remains of old cabin; Trail to Campsites #4 and #5	N40.4878 W105.4969
3.0	Trail to Campsites #6 and #7	N40.4885 W105.4993
3.1	Trail to Campsite #8	N40.4886 W105.5000
3.4	Trail to Campsite #9	N40.4910 W105.5048
4.4	Leave Wilderness and enter Rocky Mountain National Park	N40.4975 W105.5162
4.5	Trail to Boundary Creek Campsite	N40.4977 W105.5186
5.1	Trail to Kettle Tarn and Kettle Tarn Campsite	N40.4984 W105.5283
5.3	Intersection with North Boundary Trail	N40.4977 W105.5307

NORTH FORK TRAIL

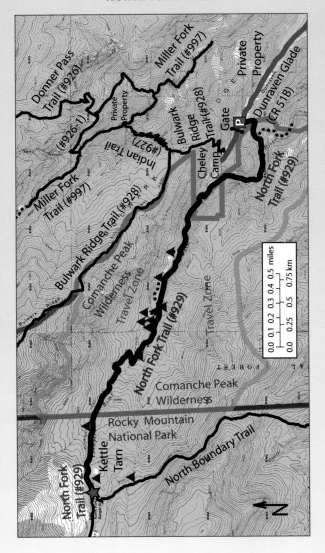

Bulwark Ridge Trail (#928)

TRAIL LENGTH	5.0 miles
TRAIL ELEVATION GAIN, LOSS, RANGE	3,100 feet, 144 feet, 8,071–11,042 feet
HIKE LENGTH	5.4 miles
HIKE ELEVATION GAIN, LOSS, RANGE	3,367 feet, 144 feet, 7,804–11,042 feet
DIFFICULTY RATING	Difficult; 12 percent average grade
STOCK RATING	Difficult
DOGS	Permitted on handheld leash within Wilderness; may not enter into National Park
SEASON	Trailhead accessible year-round; snowshoes typically necessary December–April for higher elevations
TRAILS ILLUSTRATED MAPS	Cache La Poudre/Big Thompson (#101) and Poudre River/Cameron Pass (#112)
USGS 7.5-MINUTE QUADS	Crystal Mountain, Glen Haven, and Pingree Park

COMMENT: This all-season trail provides a good full-day hike or a pleasant weekend backpacking trip. It ascends Bulwark Ridge through nearly continuous forest and a few small meadows. The long hike is well worth the effort, as it tops out at a saddle between Signal and South Signal Mountains. A short off-trail climb to either summit provides awesome panoramic views. You can look down on the rows of lower foothills and the plains to the east, while to the west the higher peaks of the Mummy Range rise majestically skyward.

GETTING THERE: From Loveland, take US 34 west for 17 miles to Drake. Turn right on Devils Gulch Road (County Road 43) and travel 6.1 miles to Dunraven Glade Road (County Road 51B). Turn right and go 2.2 miles to the Dunraven Trailhead

A group of CMC hikers heads off trail from the Bulwark Ridge Trail toward the summit of South Signal Mountain.

parking lot at the end of the public road. From the parking lot, hike west up the gated road toward Cheley Camp for 0.4 mile to the Bulwark Ridge Trailhead.

TRAIL DESCRIPTION: This trail starts by steeply climbing up onto Bulwark Ridge through a series of switchbacks. As you near the ridgeline, nice views of the surrounding mountains to the south unfold across the valley below. The trail then steadily ascends along Bulwark Ridge for the next 4.2 miles, mostly through forest, intersecting the Indian Trail at the 1.3 mile mark. (The Indian Trail branches off to the right and descends steeply down to the Miller Fork Trail.) There are a few small meadows as well, which often harbor a multitude of wild-flowers in the summer. There is no water source along this trail, so be sure to carry enough drinking water with you. As the trail crests the highpoint of Bulwark Ridge, you start to catch glimpses of Signal and South Signal Mountains ahead. The trail becomes somewhat faint along this stretch. After a short descent and another small climb, the trail reaches timberline, where it turns right and parallels treeline as it wraps around the east side of South Signal Mountain to the saddle between the two peaks. The trail becomes faint to nonexistent above timberline. The saddle is where the Bulwark Ridge Trail ends and the Signal Mountain Trail begins. There is no intersection, sign, or marker here to indicate the name change.

NEARBY OFF-TRAIL DESTINATION
SOUTH SIGNAL MOUNTAIN (5.3 miles, 3,513 feet elevation gain+loss): If you hike the Bulwark Ridge Trail to timberline, then this off-trail hike is a must! When you reach timberline, break off the trail steeply uphill, working your way around several large rock outcrops. The summit has numerous rock outcrops too. One on the west side of the summit is the high-point (N40.5188 W105.5183), but those on the east side are more fun for some easy scrambling. From the top, you have stunning views in all directions, including the high peaks of the Mummy Range to the west.

Looking toward Signal Mountain from neighboring South Signal Mountain.

BULWARK RIDGE TRAIL

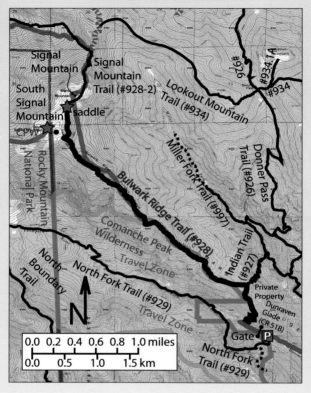

BULWARK RIDGE TRAIL		
MILEAGE	**DESTINATIONS**	**GPS WAYPOINTS**
	Dunraven Trailhead	N40.4756 W105.4605
0.4	Bulwark Ridge Trailhead (turn right)	N40.4779 W105.4665
1.3	Intersection with Indian Trail (turn left)	N40.4861 W105.4658
2.8	Wilderness boundary	N40.4973 W105.4872
5.0	Timberline	N40.5167 W105.5137
5.4	Saddle between Signal and South Signal Mountains	N40.5231 W105.5130

North Boundary Trail (NBT)

TRAIL LENGTH	5.8 miles
TRAIL ELEVATION GAIN, LOSS, RANGE	2,627 feet, 1,188 feet, 7,880–9,710 feet
HIKE LENGTH	6.1 miles
HIKE ELEVATION GAIN, LOSS, RANGE	2,682 feet, 1,203 feet, 7,830–9,710 feet
DIFFICULTY RATING	Difficult; 12 percent average grade
STOCK RATING	Difficult (no horse trailer parking at trailhead)
DOGS	Prohibited on all sections of the trail
SEASON	Trailhead accessible year-round; snowshoes typically necessary December–March
TRAILS ILLUSTRATED MAP	Rocky Mountain National Park (#200)
USGS 7.5-MINUTE QUAD	Estes Park

COMMENT: This is the only trail in the Comanche Peak Wilderness that provides access to waterfalls: West Creek Falls and Fox Creek Falls, both at the end of spur trails. The falls are most impressive in late spring and early summer, but are also beautiful when they freeze in the winter. This trail's rugged beauty and peaceful solitude, as it climbs up and down forest ridges and valleys, make it very appealing. Where the forest opens up, there are also several nice broad views.

GETTING THERE: From Loveland, take US 34 west for 17 miles to Drake. Turn right on Devils Gulch Road (County Road 43) and travel 11.5 miles, then turn right onto McGraw Ranch Road. Follow the road for 2.1 miles to the Cow Creek Trailhead. Or, from Lyons on US 36, veer onto US 34 west at the second stoplight in Estes Park. After traveling 0.4 mile, turn right onto McGregor Avenue (which becomes Devils Gulch

A view of the Mummy Range from the North Boundary Trail.

Road as it leaves town). After another 3.5 miles, turn left onto McGraw Ranch Road (there is a brown National Park sign at this intersection). Follow the road for 2.1 miles to the Cow Creek Trailhead. Parking is very limited and permitted only on the left (west) side of the road. Only passenger vehicles should attempt to use this parking area, as there is not enough room for trailers or motor homes to turn around. Horses are permitted on the trail, but equestrians will have to access the area from a different trailhead with space to park a horse trailer. From the parking area, hike up the Cow Creek Trail past the cabins for 0.3 mile to the beginning of the North Boundary Trail.

TRAIL DESCRIPTION: This trail begins and ends in Rocky Mountain National Park, but also passes through the Comanche Peak Wilderness for a good portion of its length. It starts by steeply climbing up and over a saddle to the north, shortly reaching the National Park/Wilderness boundary. At the saddle are nice views of the mountains to the north, including the top of South Signal Mountain, while dropping down from the saddle you can often find numerous dainty and beautiful Calypso Orchids in late May and early June. At the bottom of the valley, the trail crosses West Creek over a narrow footbridge and then immediately intersects the unmarked West Creek Trail, where you turn left. Shortly after that, it intersects the West Creek Falls Trail; turn left here to see the falls or turn right to stay on the North Boundary Trail. The trail then ascends up out of the valley, and provides some nice views of the Mummy Range to the west, but soon enters into

Upper West Creek Falls gushes with melt water in the early summer.

Dainty and delicate Calypso Orchids can be found along the North Boundary Trail in early summer.

denser pine forest and descends a short way down to Fox Creek. Then the trail begins another steep climb, angling up a ridge toward the north. As you near the highpoint of the trail, the forest begins to open up a bit again, providing the trail's best views of the Mummy Range to the west. For the most unobstructed views, you can cut off the trail a short distance and climb one of several rock outcrops in the area. After this point, the trail begins a more gradual descent down into the valley of the North Fork of the Big Thompson River. Early in the descent, there are views of South Signal Mountain to the north through gaps in the trees. Eventually the trail reaches a small bridge that crosses the North Fork of the Big Thompson River. Immediately before the bridge is a quaint meadow with a ranger cabin, and immediately after the river is the intersection with the North Fork Trail.

NEARBY DESTINATIONS

WEST CREEK FALLS (2.3 miles, 1,420 feet elevation gain+loss): For an interesting side trip, follow the West Creek Falls Trail west into the National Park for 0.7 mile to beautiful West Creek Falls (N40.4512 W105.5170).

FOX CREEK FALLS (2.9 miles, 2,024 feet elevation gain+loss): Immediately after crossing Fox Creek along the North Boundary Trail, turn right and follow a faint scratch trail along Fox Creek for 0.1 mile to some small cascades. Following for another 0.1 mile takes you to taller 15-foot falls (N40.4581 W105.5111). Older maps show a trail leading from the falls to the east, but we found no indication of this trail.

NORTH BOUNDARY TRAIL		
MILEAGE	**DESTINATIONS**	**GPS WAYPOINTS**
	Cow Creek Trailhead	N40.4306 W105.5006
0.3	Turn from Cow Creek Trail onto North Boundary Trail	N40.4314 W105.5033
0.4	Leave National Park and enter Comanche Peak Wilderness	N40.4338 W105.5040
0.9	Saddle	N40.4397 W105.5048
1.5	Bridge and West Creek Trail intersection (turn left)	N40.4458 W105.5049
1.7	Intersection with West Creek Falls Trail (turn right)	N40.4475 W105.5071
2.7	Fox Creek	N40.4590 W105.5128
4.2	Highpoint (9,710 feet)	N40.4780 W105.5167
5.6	Side trail to Sylvanmere Campsite	N40.4922 W105.5294
6.0	Ranger cabin	N40.4969 W105.5324
6.0	Bridge over North Fork of Big Thompson River	N40.4972 W105.5309
6.1	Intersection with North Fork Trail	N40.4977 W105.5307

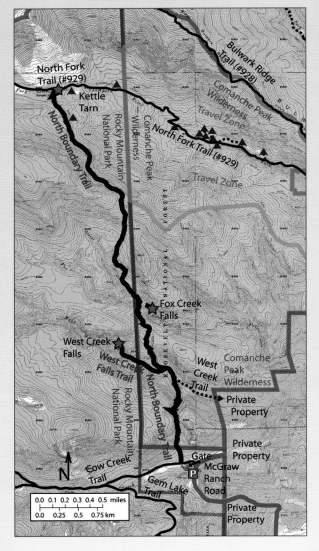

Little Beaver Creek
Trail (#948, formerly #855)

TRAIL LENGTH	7.1 miles
ELEVATION GAIN, LOSS, RANGE	1,931 feet, 280 feet, 8,052–9,797 feet
DIFFICULTY RATING	Easy; 6 percent average grade
STOCK RATING	Difficult
DOGS	Permitted on handheld leash within Wilderness
SEASON	May 15–October 31; the gate on Forest Development Road 152 is generally opened around Memorial Day, but you can hike or snowshoe up the road to the trailhead when the gate is closed
TRAILS ILLUSTRATED MAP	Poudre River/Cameron Pass (#112)
USGS 7.5-MINUTE QUADS	Kinikinik, Pingree Park, Rustic

COMMENT: This is a pleasant trail that follows along gently cascading Little Beaver Creek for much of its length. Most of the trail resides in cool, shady forest, although there are also a few meadows along the way. In fact, the highlight of the trail is beautiful Beaver Park, a grassy hillside that rises above the creek and allows a delightful view of the creek and its beaver ponds below.

GETTING THERE: From Fort Collins, take US 287 north to the intersection with Colorado 14 at Ted's Place. Then travel west on Colorado 14 for 26 miles to Pingree Park Road (County Road 63E). Turn left and travel 6.2 miles to Old Flowers Road (Forest Development Road 152). Turn right and go through Jack's Gulch Campground. On the far side of the campground is the Jack's Gulch Trailhead, which is the best place to park to hike the trail (and the only place for horse trailers). If you have a high-clearance vehicle, you can drive another 0.6 mile and

The western section of the Little Beaver Creek Trail passes through this small clearing.

try to find a place to park off the side of the road near the start of the trail, although there is not an official parking area here. The trail starts at an intersection in the road, where a sign indicates "Little Beaver Creek–1 mile."

TRAIL DESCRIPTION: The trail heads downhill through a meadow to a small footbridge over a creek before leveling off and entering mostly open forest. After a short distance, it crosses another small creek (which may be dry during some parts of the year), and shortly thereafter you'll come upon a wire gate at the boundary of the Comanche Peak Wilderness (note, this boundary is slightly south of where maps indicate it to be). Please make sure that you close the gate after you, as there are sometimes free-range cattle in the area. From here, the trail works its way over to Little Beaver Creek, which it follows mostly through forest, although there are also occasional small meadows. At times, the valley narrows, so the trail climbs steeply up the side of the valley for a short distance before descending back down again once it becomes wide enough. There are three intersections along this stretch with unnamed trails. Turn right at the first two and left at the third one. There are numerous beaver dams along the creek, both old and new. The highlight of the trail is Beaver Park, where a grassy hillside overlooks beaver ponds below and provides a glimpse of Crown Point to the west. The trail intersects the Flowers Trail at two places in this meadow. It then continues on to the northwest up another drainage, eventually ending at an intersection with the faint remnants of the unmaintained Upper Dadd Gulch Trail.

Beaver ponds and a grassy hillside make Beaver Park a lovely destination.

Colorado Columbine, Golden Banner, and many other flowers can be found along the Little Beaver Creek Trail.

	LITTLE BEAVER CREEK TRAIL	
MILEAGE	**DESTINATIONS**	**GPS WAYPOINTS**
	Jack's Gulch Trailhead	N40.6344 W105.5316
	Beginning of trail	N40.6299 W105.5391
0.1	Cross footbridge over small creek	N40.6291 W105.5383
0.3	Cross Jack's Gulch creek (no bridge)	N40.6256 W105.5387
0.5	Through gate to enter Comanche Peak Wilderness	N40.6239 W105.5376
1.1	Footbridge over Little Beaver Creek	N40.6184 W105.5408
1.1	Intersection with unnamed trail (turn right)	N40.6187 W105.5405
1.3	Intersection with shortcut trail to Fish Creek Trail	N40.6166 W105.5438
1.7	Footbridge over Little Beaver Creek	N40.6175 W105.5481
2.7	Intersection with unnamed trail that returns to Old Flowers Road (turn left)	N40.6229 W105.5644
5.7	Beaver Park and intersection with Flowers Trail	N40.6383 W105.6109
7.1	Junction with unmaintained Upper Dadd Gulch Trail	N40.6506 W105.6266

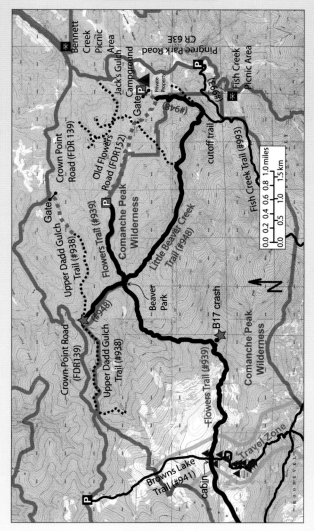

Flowers Trail (#939)

TRAIL LENGTH	15.0 miles
ELEVATION GAIN, LOSS, RANGE	3,407 feet, 2,876 feet, 8,895–11,318 feet
DIFFICULTY RATING	Difficult; 8 percent average grade
STOCK RATING	Difficult
DOGS	Permitted on handheld leash within Wilderness
SEASON	Early June through late October; the gate on Old Flowers Road (Forest Development Road 152) is generally opened around Memorial Day; deep snow is usually encountered at high elevations into June
TRAILS ILLUSTRATED MAP	Poudre River/Cameron Pass (#112)
USGS 7.5-MINUTE QUADS	Chambers Lake, Comanche Peak, Kinikinik, and Rustic

COMMENT: This is by far the longest trail in the Comanche Peak Wilderness, and it is ideal for those who want to see it all: dense quiet forests, gently burbling streams, sweeping panoramic views, sheltered mountain lakes, small grassy meadows, and delicate alpine flowers. This trail follows an old pioneer road that early travelers used to cross over these mountains; most traces of the road have disappeared, although there are still the remains of a few cabins and a wooden corral along the way. A multiday backpacking trip is required to see it all, but you can easily do a day hike to many of the destinations along this trail.

GETTING THERE: From Fort Collins, take US 287 north to the intersection with Colorado 14 at Ted's Place. Then travel west on Colorado 14 for 26 miles to Pingree Park Road (County Road 63E). Turn left and travel 6.2 miles to Old Flowers Road (Forest Development Road 152). Turn right and go through Jack's Gulch Campground. On the far side of the campground

Looking down on Browns and Timberline Lakes from the Flowers Trail.

is a parking lot, which is the best place to park for those with low-clearance vehicles (and the only place for horse trailers). If you have a high-clearance vehicle, you can drive 3 miles on Old Flowers Road to its end, where there is a small parking area (not big enough for trailers to turn around).

TRAIL DESCRIPTION: This trail follows an old road surveyed and developed by Jacob Flowers in 1879. It was built to allow access to broad expanses of mountain timber, as well as to provide a route between Fort Collins and the town of Walden in North Park. The trail ascends up to a small pass through mostly lodgepole pine forest. After the pass, the trail descends rather steeply down to Beaver Park, a nice hillside meadow overlooking a series of beaver ponds along Little Beaver Creek.

Beaver Park is one of many wonderful destinations along the Flowers Trail.

There are two intersections with the Little Beaver Creek Trail in this small park. The trail then travels through a long tree tunnel as it steadily climbs toward timberline. At about the 5.5 mile mark, the trail pops up out of the trees, providing great views of the higher peaks of the Mummy Range to the south. Over the next 5 miles, the trail travels near timberline, although it mainly stays below it. Shortly before intersecting the Browns Lake Trail, it enters a USFS Travel Zone, where camping is allowed only in designated sites. One site is situated a little distance before the intersection, while the other is a short distance after. The remains of an old cabin can be seen along a small creek near the intersection. About 1 mile later, the trail passes by an overlook—a highlight of the trail—with views down into the cirque holding Browns and Timberline Lakes. Eventually, the trail intersects the Beaver Creek and Zimmerman Trails. Just to the northwest of the Beaver Creek Trail intersection are the remnants of an old corral or pen, and a couple hundred yards to the south, on the Beaver Creek Trail, there are the remains of an old sheepherder's cabin. The Flowers Trail continues on to the west, but becomes increasingly faint as it crosses the alpine tundra, eventually becoming just a series of cairns with no path at all, and ultimately disappearing entirely. Along this stretch there are beautiful views of the Medicine Bow Range to the northwest and the Never Summer Range to the west and southwest. Soon, the trail begins a drop below timberline, descending almost 3,000 feet in 3.5 miles to the Big South Trail. This section of trail is so faint that it is very difficult to distinguish it from the multitude of faint animal trails that crisscross through the forest. This section of trail should only

The Flowers Trail crosses over Little Beaver Creek shortly past Beaver Park.

be attempted by those with good orienteering skills. The trail ends at an intersection with the Big South Trail immediately below the site of a washed-out bridge that used to cross the Big South Fork of the Cache la Poudre River.

NEARBY OFF-TRAIL DESTINATION

CROWN POINT B-17 CRASH SITE (4.8 miles, 2,566 feet elevation gain+loss): On the night of June 13, 1944, a B-17 bomber crashed into the mountainside while on a training mission, killing four of the ten onboard. The cause of the crash was an incorrect position estimate. To get to the crash site, follow the Flowers Trail southwest from Beaver Park for 2.8 miles; at a sharp right-hand turn in the trail, a faint path leaves to the left. Follow this path to the east 0.2 mile to the crash site (N40.6121 W105.6333). Out of respect for the families of the fallen soldiers and for those who will visit this site in the future, please do not remove or touch any of the debris. Much of the debris from the plane crash remains, scattered over an area of about 2,500 square yards, although from what we've been told, many of the more interesting artifacts have already been removed by thoughtless hikers.

FLOWERS TRAIL		
MILEAGE	**DESTINATIONS**	**GPS WAYPOINTS**
	Jack's Gulch Trailhead	N40.6344 W105.5316
	Flowers Trailhead	N40.6437 W105.5813
1.1	Pass	N40.6424 W105.6009
1.8	Beaver Park and intersection with Little Beaver Creek Trail	N40.6388 W105.6114
4.6	Turnoff to B-17 crash site	N40.6123 W105.6361
7.4	Browns Lake Trail	N40.6131 W105.6813
8.2	Browns and Timberline Lakes overlook	N40.6122 W105.6912
10.1	Beaver Creek Trail intersection	N40.5939 W105.7183
10.2	Zimmerman Trail intersection	N40.5932 W105.7210
11.7	Mirror Lake Trail intersection (undefined)	N40.5823 W105.7421
15.0	Big South Trail intersection	N40.5567 W105.7788

FLOWERS TRAIL WEST

(for Flowers Trail East Section, see map on page 39)

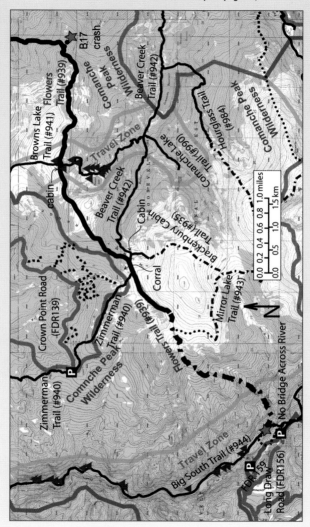

Fish Creek Trail (#993, formerly #1009)

TRAIL LENGTH	6.4 miles
ELEVATION GAIN, LOSS, RANGE	1,618 feet, 442 feet, 7,910–9,186 feet
DIFFICULTY RATING	Easy; 6 percent average grade
STOCK RATING	Easy
DOGS	Permitted on handheld leash within Wilderness
SEASON	Trailhead accessible year-round; snowshoes typically necessary December–April
TRAILS ILLUSTRATED MAP	Poudre River/Cameron Pass (#112)
USGS 7.5-MINUTE QUAD	Pingree Park

COMMENT: This trail provides a cool, shady hike on a hot summer day, or an out-of-the-wind snowshoe in the wintertime. It follows its namesake for almost half its length, but it starts with a climb up and over a forested ridge that allows glimpses of the alpine peaks of the Mummy Range to the south. And near the end of the trail, you pass through one of the darkest stretches of forest we have encountered in the Comanche Peak Wilderness.

GETTING THERE

FISH CREEK TRAILHEAD: From Fort Collins, take US 287 north to the intersection with Colorado 14 at Ted's Place. Then travel west on Colorado 14 for 26 miles to Pingree Park Road (County Road 63E). Turn left and travel 7.7 miles to the Fish Creek Trailhead, which is along the right side of the road. The parking area here only has room for three vehicles, but there is space for additional vehicles just beyond the bridge across the Little South Fork of the Cache la Poudre River.

BEAVER CREEK TRAILHEAD: See Beaver Creek Trail description.

TRAIL DESCRIPTION: This trail ascends steeply along a ridge that sits between Fish and Little Beaver Creeks. There are

A grove of aspen near the highpoint of the Fish Creek Trail.

occasional glimpses of the high peaks of the Mummy Range through the ponderosa pine and aspen trees along this ridge. After reaching the highpoint of the ridge, the trail begins to descend the other side, intersecting a cutoff trail to the Little Beaver Creek Trail at a saddle. From here, it continues to descend down to Fish Creek, and then follows the softly cascading creek for the next 2.7 miles. The trail ranges from just along the bank of the creek to 50 yards away, and passes through several small meadows. Immediately after crossing a bridge over the creek, the trail works its way up a side drainage under dark, dense forest. As it climbs out of this drainage, the forest starts to become more open. The trail ends after a short descent down to the Beaver Creek Trailhead parking lot on

One of several small meadows along the Fish Creek Trail.

Forest Development Road 145, just below the Sky Ranch Camp. Snowshoeing this trail requires good orienteering skills, as it is often hard to see the trail when it is covered with snow, especially in the meadows.

	FISH CREEK TRAIL	
MILEAGE	DESTINATIONS	GPS WAYPOINTS
	Fish Creek Trailhead	N40.6185 W105.5258
1.0	Enter Comanche Peak Wilderness	N40.6161 W105.5356
1.3	Reach top of ridge	N40.6144 W105.5394
1.8	Intersection with shortcut trail to Little Beaver Creek Trail (turn left)	N40.6108 W105.5465
2.4	Reach Fish Creek	N40.6035 W105.5493
5.1	Cross bridge over Fish Creek	N40.5943 W105.5945
5.9	Leave Comanche Peak Wilderness	N40.5860 W105.5949
6.3	Intersection with unnamed trail (turn right)	N40.5818 W105.5981
6.4	Beaver Creek Trailhead on FDR 145	N40.5804 W105.6004

FISH CREEK TRAIL

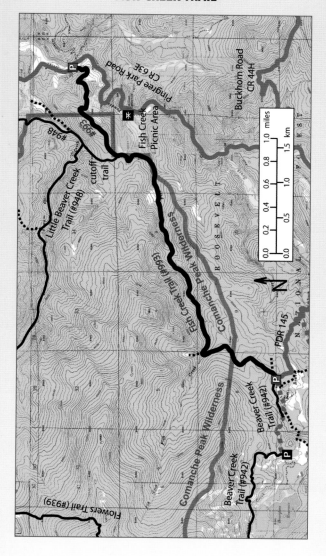

Signal Mountain Trail (#928-2)

TRAIL LENGTH	6.0 miles
ELEVATION GAIN, LOSS, RANGE	2,706 feet, 398 feet, 8,476–11,200 feet
DIFFICULTY RATING	Difficult; 10 percent average grade
STOCK RATING	Difficult
DOGS	Permitted on handheld leash within Wilderness
SEASON	Trailhead accessible year-round; snowshoes typically necessary December–May
TRAILS ILLUSTRATED MAP	Poudre River/Cameron Pass (#112)
USGS 7.5-MINUTE QUAD	Pingree Park

COMMENT: This trail provides a variety of hiking and scenery. The lower portion of the trail follows the pleasant banks of Pennock Creek through shady forest at the bottom of a deep valley, while the upper portion tops out on the alpine tundra on the flank of Signal Mountain. It also passes by one of the more striking monoliths you'll ever see in Colorado.

GETTING THERE: From Fort Collins, take US 287 north to the intersection with Colorado 14 at Ted's Place. Then travel west on Colorado 14 for 26 miles to Pingree Park Road (County Road 63E). Turn left and travel 13.1 miles to the Signal Mountain Trailhead: a small pull-off along the west side of the road that can only hold about three vehicles.

TRAIL DESCRIPTION: The trail starts with a short, steep descent down into a small valley, makes a gradual climb around a ridge, and then drops down into the larger, steep-sided Pennock Creek Valley. At the bottom of the valley, you can see where the trail used to come in from the left (shown on older topographic maps). Don't follow this old trail, as it passes through private property. Instead, turn right, and follow the

The Signal Mountain Trail passes beneath this 80-foot-tall monolith that resembles a stone giant. Hikers at its base provide scale.

trail upstream along the creek for the next 3.5 miles. A short distance up the valley, you'll pass by the remnants of two small cabins on the right. Look carefully, as it's easy to miss them. This hike along the creek would be great even if that was all there was to see; in some places the creek tumbles and splashes through a series of small cascades, while in other areas it flows gently through small meadows. Eventually, though, the trail climbs out of the valley. Suddenly, you'll discover that you are passing beneath a tall monolith that resembles a storybook giant. It rises to a height of 80 feet,

Signal Mountain provides a breathtaking view of the higher peaks of the Mummy Range to the west.

seemingly out of nowhere, making you wonder why this enormous rock is there all by itself. After the monolith, the trail begins to steepen considerably up to a small pass. At the pass, the trail intersects the Lookout Mountain Trail, where you'll turn right to continue on the Signal Mountain Trail. The Lookout Mountain Trail makes for a nice hike too, eventually reaching its namesake outside the Comanche Peak Wilderness. The trail continues a steep ascent to the south, eventually breaking above timberline. From timberline, it's only 0.25 mile and 300 feet of elevation gain across beautiful alpine tundra to the high point of the trail on the east flank of Signal Mountain. The top of the trail provides beautiful views to the east of a multitude of lower peaks. But make sure you look down by your feet too, as there is a wide variety of wildflowers in this area in the summer. The final portion of the trail is quite faint and descends down to the saddle between Signal and South Signal Mountains. The saddle is where the Signal Mountain Trail ends and the Bulwark Ridge Trail begins. There is no intersection, sign, or marker here to indicate the name change.

NEARBY OFF-TRAIL DESTINATION
SIGNAL MOUNTAIN (5.7 miles, 2,767 feet elevation gain+loss): If you hike the Signal Mountain Trail to timberline, then this

off-trail hike to the summit is a must! Follow the trail until just before it starts to descend down to the saddle between the two mountains. From this point, the summit is only 200 yards horizontally and 60 feet vertically to the west. From the top, you have panoramic views of the Wilderness, including the high peaks of the Mummy Range to the west.

	SIGNAL MOUNTAIN TRAIL	
MILEAGE	**DESTINATIONS**	**GPS WAYPOINTS**
	Signal Mountain Trailhead	N40.5665 W105.5552
0.5	Pass by old cabins	N40.5653 W105.5503
0.7	Bridge	N40.5626 W105.5480
2.0	Enter Comanche Peak Wilderness	N40.5495 W105.5515
2.6	Collapsed bridge	N40.5455 W105.5433
3.9	Leave Pennock Creek	N40.5397 W105.5206
4.6	Monolith	N40.5372 W105.5111
4.9	Intersection with Lookout Mountain Trail (turn right)	N40.5346 W105.5068
5.4	Timberline	N40.5295 W105.5085
5.7	Trail high point	N40.5254 W105.5096
6.0	Saddle	N40.5231 W105.5130

SIGNAL MOUNTAIN TRAIL

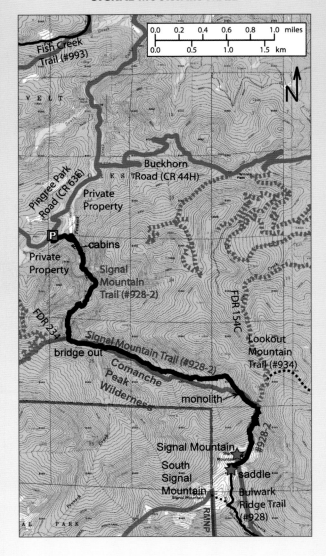

Stormy Peaks Trail (#980)

TRAIL LENGTH	5.2 miles
ELEVATION GAIN, LOSS, RANGE	2,673 feet, 30 feet, 9,017–11,667 feet
DIFFICULTY RATING	Difficult; 10 percent average grade
STOCK RATING	Difficult
DOGS	Permitted on handheld leash within Wilderness up to National Park boundary
SEASON	Trailhead accessible year-round; snowshoes typically necessary December through early June
TRAILS ILLUSTRATED MAP	Poudre River/Cameron Pass (#112)
USGS 7.5-MINUTE QUAD	Pingree Park

COMMENT: This four-season trail offers a wide range of hikes, some of which involve following unofficial side trails (shown on the map). The trail itself passes through mostly evergreen forest, with a couple of nice views looking down on Pingree Park along the way. Eventually, it climbs above timberline into Rocky Mountain National Park, and passes through delicate alpine tundra, topping out at Stormy Peaks Pass.

GETTING THERE: From Fort Collins, take US 287 north to the intersection with Colorado 14 at Ted's Place. Travel west on Colorado 14 for 26 miles to Pingree Park Road (County Road 63E). Turn left and go 15.9 miles to Pingree Park. As you approach Pingree Park, there is a fork in the road; veer left and drive 150 yards to the trailhead, which is on the left side of the road.

TRAIL DESCRIPTION: The first 0.25 mile of the trail passes through a forest of small aspen and pine trees that have grown up since the 1994 Hourglass Fire that destroyed much of Colorado State University's Pingree Park campus. It then climbs gradually toward the south through dense evergreen

Fog can be seen rolling up the valley below from the Stormy Peaks Trail.

forest, passing the Denny's Point and Twin Lakes Trails along the way. Each of these side trails is short and provides a closer destination for those seeking a shorter hike. The trail begins to climb more steeply as it enters the Comanche Peak Wilderness. Shortly after the Wilderness boundary, there is a great overlook of Pingree Park, as well as a view of the towering mountains above. The hike would be worth doing if this were the final destination, but there are even better views to come. About a mile after entering the Wilderness, the trail enters Rocky Mountain National Park. If you have a dog along on the hike, this is where you must turn around, as dogs are not allowed on trails in the Park. The trail continues its steady ascent past a National Park backcountry campsite (reservations necessary) and up above timberline. The views above timberline are spectacular, with peaks towering above in many directions, and in early to mid-summer, a multitude of wildflowers flourish in this area. The trail makes its way along the north side of a valley up to Stormy Peaks Pass. This is where the hike described here ends, but the trail continues on from the pass, descending 1.8 miles, steeply at times, to its end at the Lost Lake Trail.

NEARBY OFF-TRAIL DESTINATIONS

PINGREE PARK B-17 CRASH SITE (3.0 miles, 1,299 feet elevation gain+loss): On the night of October 18, 1943, a B-17 bomber crashed into the side of Stormy Peaks while on a training mission, killing all eight onboard. The cause of the crash was an incorrect position estimate. To get to the crash site, follow the Stormy Peaks Trail and turn left at the sign indicating the way to Twin Lakes Reservoir (N40.5634 W105.5847). After reaching the reservoir, follow the old road/trail south along the western side of the reservoir past a gate blocking the road/trail (N40.5606 W105.5830). At a fork in the road/trail, turn left uphill (N40.5558 W105.5866). At another intersection, where three posts block the road/trail, veer left (N40.5529 W105.5852). A sign indicates where you enter the Wilderness (N40.5508 W105.5843). At a saddle, the road/trail narrows

Moose are frequently seen along and near the trails in the Pingree Park area.

(N40.5484 W105.5827). From here the trail follows a canal that diverts water across the saddle from a creek on the other side. At the intersection of the creek and canal is a water diversion structure; keep the same general heading past the creek. Shortly after, the trail intersects the end of an old logging road. About 30 yards down the road, turn right onto a faint trail (N40.5439 W105.5800). At the end of the trail is the crash site, located at the base of a rocky ridge (N40.5402 W105.5764). Out of respect for the families of the fallen soldiers and for those who will visit this site in the future, please do not remove or touch any of the debris. Much of the debris from the plane crash has been removed, but larger pieces still remain, scattered over an area about the size of a football field.

STORMY PEAKS (5.4 miles, 3,140 feet elevation gain+loss): Follow the Stormy Peaks Trail more than 4 miles to where it ascends above timberline. When you get to a position due west of a saddle on the northwest side of Stormy Peaks (N40.5236 W105.5957), cut off-trail toward the saddle, making sure to minimize your impact on the alpine tundra. From the saddle (N40.5238 W105.5903), the easiest approach is to curve around and ascend the northeast slope to the rocky summit (N40.5198 W105.5868). From the summit, there are great views of many of the lower peaks to the northeast, as well as a better view of much of the rest of the Mummy Range to the southwest.

STORMY PEAKS TRAIL		
MILEAGE **DESTINATIONS**		**GPS WAYPOINTS**
	Stormy Peaks Trailhead	N40.5704 W105.5883
0.5	Intersection with Denny's Point Trail (turn right)	N40.5661 W105.5860
0.7	Intersection with Twin Lakes Trail (turn right)	N40.5634 W105.5847
2.3	Comanche Peak Wilderness boundary	N40.5479 W105.6014
3.2	Rocky Mountain National Park boundary	N40.5387 W105.6089
4.0	Stormy Peaks North backcountry campsite	N40.5290 W105.6035
5.2	Stormy Peaks Pass	N40.5165 W105.5892

STORMY PEAKS TRAIL

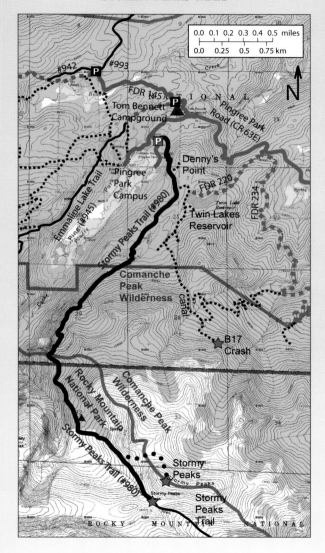

Emmaline Lake Trail

(#945, formerly #854)

TRAIL LENGTH	5.9 miles
ELEVATION GAIN, LOSS, RANGE	2,128 feet, 50 feet, 8,958–11,015 feet
DIFFICULTY RATING	Moderate; 7 percent average grade
STOCK RATING	Easy (permitted up to USFS Travel Zone boundary)
DOGS	Permitted on handheld leash within Wilderness
SEASON	Mid-June through late October; trailhead generally accessible around mid-June, although you can hike or snowshoe up Forest Development Road 145 to the trailhead year-round
TRAILS ILLUSTRATED MAP	Poudre River/Cameron Pass (#112)
USGS 7.5-MINUTE QUADS	Comanche Peak and Pingree Park

COMMENT: This trail provides a wide variety of scenery. It passes through the charred remains of the 1994 Hourglass Fire, which is filling up with new life, then enters dense, cool forest and emerges into Cirque Meadow: a beautiful swampy meadow that allows impressive views of the snow-fringed peaks to the southwest. It tops out at timberline, where picturesque Cirque and Emmaline Lakes lie in a deep cirque beneath Comanche Peak and Fall Mountain.

GETTING THERE: From Fort Collins, take US 287 north to the intersection with Colorado 14 at Ted's Place. Travel west on Colorado 14 for 26 miles to Pingree Park Road (County Road 63E). Turn left and go 15.4 miles to the turnoff to Tom Bennett Campground (Forest Development Road 145). Follow FDR 145 for 0.2 mile past the campground to the Emmaline Lake Trailhead, which has parking for only about five vehicles, although there are several pull-offs nearby along the road.

The lower section of the Emmaline Lake Trail follows an old logging road through occasional stands of aspen.

TRAIL DESCRIPTION: This trail is easy up to Cirque Meadow; it slowly ascends a relatively smooth old forest access road to the meadow. In fact, you can drive the first 0.5 mile of the trail to a gate in a high-clearance vehicle, but the trail is a bit too narrow for larger vehicles and there is very little parking space by the gate, so we suggest that you hike it. The first 1.25 miles of the trail pass through a burn area from the Hourglass Fire that destroyed 80 percent of the Pingree Park campus. There are intersections with two small trails along this stretch; go straight at both intersections. The trail then enters into forest that wasn't affected by the fire and crosses two short bridges over a small pond along Fall Creek. Be sure to look for trout in the clear water of the pond. Just before and after the bridges are two unmarked trail intersections. About 0.3 mile later, the Mummy Pass Trail departs to the left, while there is an established USFS campsite with a metal fire ring to the right of the trail. Beyond this intersection, there is another mile of shady trail through the forest, until Cirque Meadow is reached. The meadow is about 400 yards long and 200 yards wide, with a dam at the near end, partially flooding it. Here a bridge crosses over Fall Creek as the trail wraps around the north side of the meadow. Another trail goes along the south side of the meadow, leading to four established USFS campsites with metal fire rings. These campsites, along with two other established campsites just before the meadow, are outside of the Wilderness and the USFS Travel Zone, and are a good place for those on horseback to spend the night, as stock animals are prohibited from entering this Travel Zone. The trail continues another 2.3 miles, as it ascends to Cirque and Emmaline Lakes, resting at treeline below towering Comanche Peak and Fall Mountain. For the final two miles, the trail is quite rocky and crosses several streams and numerous boggy areas, where log bridges are provided. The trail also becomes faint in spots, so look carefully for the tree blazes and rock cairns that mark the way.

Looking down from Comanche Peak on little Emmaline and Cirque Lakes.

Cirque Meadow lies about midway up the Emmaline Lake Trail and provides an impressive view of the higher peaks ahead.

NEARBY OFF-TRAIL DESTINATION

COMANCHE PEAK (6.4 miles, 3,956 feet elevation gain+loss): Comanche Peak is the highest named* summit in the Comanche Peak Wilderness. At the intersection with the Old Morrill Trail (where a sign indicates to turn right to Surprise Pond), turn right and follow the trail as it winds its way through the remnants of the Hourglass Fire, turning left at intersections with the Sky Ranch Cutoff Trail (N40.5680 W105.6051) and the Beaver Falls Trail (N40.5676 W105.6062) and then right at the intersection with the Surprise Pond Trail (N40.5619 W105.6117), where a sign says "Comanche Peak—Trail Incomplete." The trail becomes fainter as you climb the western ridge of Comanche Peak, but occasional cairns should help you follow it up to near timberline and an outcrop dubbed locally as "Golgotha." Above timberline, continue to follow the ridgeline, eventually making it to the summit (N40.5482 W105.6766) after a long, steady, and grueling climb. The location of the summit benchmark on the map is the easternmost of three rock outcrops on the summit area, while the true summit is located atop the westernmost bump.

---

*Although Comanche Peak is the highest named summit in the Wilderness, the highest point, by a few feet, is located 0.5 mile to the west at a point mislabeled as 12,681 feet. Its actual height based on its benchmark elevation is 12,716 feet.

The summit provides amazing views in all directions. For an extra-long day, this peak can be combined with Fall Mountain, as it is an easy 1.7-mile hike between the two across gently sloping alpine tundra. (See the Fall Mountain description for details on descending by this other route.)

EMMALINE LAKE TRAIL		
MILEAGE	**DESTINATIONS**	**GPS WAYPOINTS**
	Emmaline Lake Trailhead	N40.5764 W105.5843
0.6	Intersection with Sky Ranch Trail (go straight)	N40.5707 W105.5975
1.1	Intersection with Old Morrill/Surprise Pond Trail (go straight)	N40.5677 W105.5997
2.1	Intersection with Surprise Pond Trail (unmarked)	N40.5577 W105.6112
2.1	Cross small bridges over Fall Creek	N40.5575 W105.6112
2.4	Intersection with Mummy Pass Trail (go straight)	N40.5563 W105.6149
3.4	Cirque Meadow; cross bridge over Fall Creek	N40.5515 W105.6270
3.8	Comanche Peak Wilderness boundary	N40.5501 W105.6333
4.8	Enter Travel Zone	N40.5464 W105.6488
5.7	Cirque Lake	N40.5412 W105.6613
5.9	End of trail at Emmaline Lake	N40.5426 W105.6614

CAMPSITES

#1 "Y" Campsite	N40.5564 W105.6150
#2 Spruce Campsite	N40.5513 W105.6266
#3 Pine Campsite	N40.5510 W105.6270
#4 Fir Campsite	N40.5508 W105.6278
#5 Aspen Campsite	N40.5503 W105.6278
#6 Juniper Campsite	N40.5521 W105.6273
#7 Willow Campsite	N40.5518 W105.6281
Travel Zone Campsite #1	N40.5494 W105.6344
Travel Zone Campsite #2	N40.5497 W105.6346
Travel Zone Campsite #3	N40.5460 W105.6443
Travel Zone Campsite #4	N40.5464 W105.6473

EMMALINE LAKE TRAIL

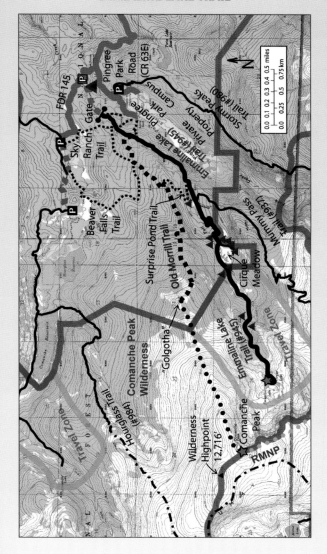

Mummy Pass Trail (#937)

TRAIL LENGTH	4.8 miles
TRAIL ELEVATION GAIN, LOSS, RANGE	2,120 feet, 367 feet, 9,523–11,461 feet
HIKE LENGTH	7.2 miles
HIKE ELEVATION GAIN, LOSS, RANGE	2,704 feet, 409 feet, 8,958–11,461 feet
DIFFICULTY RATING	Moderate; 8 percent average grade
STOCK RATING	Difficult
DOGS	Permitted on handheld leash within Wilderness up to National Park boundary
SEASON	Mid-June through late October; trailhead generally accessible around mid-June, but you can hike or snowshoe up Forest Development Road 145 to the Emmaline Lake Trailhead year-round
TRAILS ILLUSTRATED MAP	Poudre River/Cameron Pass (#112)
USGS 7.5-MINUTE QUADS	Comanche Peak and Pingree Park

COMMENT: If you love to hike across open alpine tundra with views in every direction, this trail is for you. The trail branches off the Emmaline Lake Trail 2.5 miles from the Emmaline Lake Trailhead. Following a forested ridgeline, it climbs above timberline and tops out on a narrow alpine plateau. Once on the plateau, it is a relatively level hike, as the trail makes its way around the east side of Fall Mountain and gently drops down to Mummy Pass. A profusion of alpine wildflowers line the trail in the summer.

GETTING THERE: From Fort Collins, take US 287 north to the intersection with Colorado 14 at Ted's Place. Travel west on Colorado 14 for 26 miles to Pingree Park Road (County Road 63E). Turn left and go 15.4 miles to the turnoff to Tom Bennett

Windblown snow covers the Mummy Pass Trail in this early-winter photo.

Campground (Forest Development Road 145). Follow FDR 145 for 0.2 mile past the campground to the Emmaline Lake Trailhead, which has parking for only about five vehicles, although there are several pull-offs nearby along the road. Then hike up the Emmaline Lake Trail for 2.4 miles to the start of the Mummy Pass Trail.

TRAIL DESCRIPTION: From its beginning at the Emmaline Lake Trail intersection, the Mummy Pass Trail makes a moderately steep climb along a forested ridgeline leading up to Fall Mountain. This portion of the trail is a tree tunnel and can be a little monotonous, but it is well worth doing because of what comes later. As the trail nears timberline, it begins a series of switchbacks up the increasingly steep slope, and passes through some interesting boulder outcrops. After a bit, it begins to level off at the National Park boundary (where dogs and their owners must turn around). From here, there are sweeping views toward the northwest of numerous lower mountains. You can also see Fall Mountain and Sugarloaf Mountain towering to either side, while the trail passes through relatively flat terrain in between. The rest of the trail to Mummy Pass goes through a series of gradual ups and downs, passing near a couple of picturesque ponds along the way. Marmots are often seen in the area, and alpine wildflowers abound. The end destination for this hike, Mummy Pass, provides views of many of the towering peaks of the Mummy Range in nearly every direction. The hike ends at the pass, but the trail continues on for another 5 miles in Rocky Mountain National Park.

NEARBY OFF-TRAIL DESTINATION

FALL MOUNTAIN (6.9 miles round-trip, 3,500 feet elevation gain+loss): This route is the most difficult of any route described in this book, and should only be attempted by those experienced in navigating up a talus slope. For those seeking a safer route, an approach can be made up the southern slope of the mountain from Mummy Pass or from Comanche Peak; however, this adds several miles round-trip to the hike. As the Mummy Pass Trail begins to level off, the eastern sub-summit of Fall Mountain comes into view. Try to visually scout out a route up from here. Once you reach the base of this mountain, turn

Plenty of snow still surrounds a small alpine pool in this late-June photo from the Mummy Pass Trail.

Looking down on lush Cirque Meadow from the Mummy Pass Trail.

right off the trail and begin to ascend the northeastern ridgeline. Generally follow the ridgeline, picking your way through the boulders, and veering slightly to the south of the sub-summit. Be very careful not to get too close to the shear northern edge of the mountain. After working your way past the sub-summit, it is a relatively easy stroll over to the actual summit (N40.5284 W105.6614), which provides beautiful views in every direction, as well as an awesome view down into the cirque below. For an extra-long day, this peak can be combined with Comanche Peak, as it is an easy 1.7-mile hike between the two across gently sloping alpine tundra. (See the Comanche Peak description for details on descending by this other route.)

	MUMMY PASS TRAIL	
MILEAGE	**DESTINATIONS**	**GPS WAYPOINTS**
	Mummy Pass Trail intersection with Emmaline Lake Trail	N40.5563 W105.6149
0.5	Wilderness boundary	N40.5517 W105.6181
3.3	National Park boundary	N40.5325 W105.6442
4.8	Mummy Pass	N40.5177 W105.6650

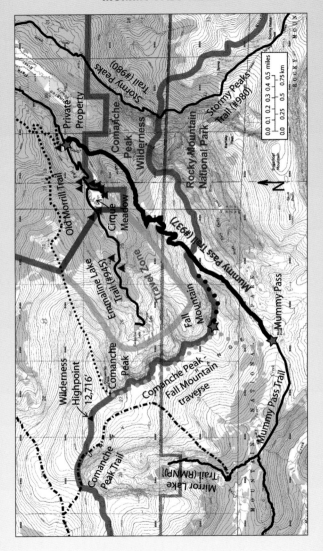

Beaver Creek Trail (#942)

TRAIL LENGTH	7.7 miles
ELEVATION GAIN, LOSS, RANGE	2,707 feet, 599 feet, 9,103–11,128 feet
DIFFICULTY RATING	Moderate; 8 percent average grade
STOCK RATING	Difficult
DOGS	Permitted on handheld leash within Wilderness
SEASON	Mid-June through late October; road to the trailhead closed due to snow in the off-season
TRAILS ILLUSTRATED MAP	Poudre River/Cameron Pass (#112)
USGS 7.5-MINUTE QUADS	Comanche Peak and Pingree Park

COMMENT: If what you're looking for is a quiet hike in the forest, then this is the trail for you. However, you'll see more than trees along this trail. Naturally, it follows its namesake, gently burbling Beaver Creek, for much of its length. It also passes through some scree above the largest lake in the area, Comanche Reservoir. Finally, it tops out near an alpine ridge, where panoramic views and delicate flowers abound.

Beaver Creek is relatively calm along this lower stretch of the Beaver Creek Trail.

View of the Medicine Bow Range a short distance to the west of the end of the Beaver Creek Trail.

GETTING THERE: From Fort Collins, take US 287 north to the intersection with Colorado 14 at Ted's Place. Travel west on Colorado 14 for 26 miles to Pingree Park Road (County Road 63E). Turn left and travel 15.4 miles to the turnoff to Tom Bennett Campground (Forest Development Road 145). Follow FDR 145 for 1.3 miles to the trailhead just before Sky Ranch Camp (see Emmaline Lake Trail map). If the gate at the ranch is open (which it is almost all summer), you can drive another 1.2 miles to the second trailhead, but be aware that they sometimes close the gate if no one is at the camp, particularly outside the summer months. The trail from the first trailhead works its way around the camp and then rejoins FDR 145 to the second trailhead.

TRAIL DESCRIPTION: The first section of trail between Trailheads 1 and 2 is mostly level and passes through pine forest, skirting along the north side of Sky Ranch Camp. After rejoining the road, it soon reaches the second trailhead. From

here, the trail starts by climbing slightly uphill to the north through lodgepole pine forest in order to go around the private land around Hourglass Reservoir, before turning west along the northern edge of the private property. This stretch isn't particularly exciting, although you do get a couple of glimpses of Hourglass Reservoir below. After a bit, the trail begins to

Frédérique and friends Mary Jackson and Manuel Fillon hike up the Beaver Creek Trail.

head downhill and eventually runs along Beaver Creek. After a short distance, the trail passes by Comanche Reservoir by climbing the ridge to its north a couple hundred feet above the lake, providing great views of the reservoir and the surrounding area. It then descends back down to lake level as it reaches the western end of the reservoir and then parallels Beaver Creek about 100 yards away. Shortly after, the trail enters a USFS Travel Zone in somewhat open forest and intersects both the Browns Lake and Comanche Lake Trails. After these intersections, the trail begins to climb more steadily to the west through dense forest for the next 3 miles up to timberline, as it follows the creek generally about 50 yards away. Just below timberline are the remains of an old sheepherder's cabin near a small pond, where the trail intersects the Brackenbury Cabin Trail. A short distance farther, the trail climbs above timberline to its end at the intersection with the Flowers Trail. Just beyond the Flowers Trail are the remnants of two old corrals, while a very short distance west on the Flowers Trail you will top out on a ridge and be greeted with a beautiful view of the Medicine Bow Range to the northwest.

BEAVER CREEK TRAIL		
MILEAGE	**DESTINATIONS**	**GPS WAYPOINTS**
	Beaver Creek Trailhead #1	N40.5810 W105.6002
0.6	Trail joins FDR 145	N40.5798 W105.6098
1.1	Hourglass/Beaver Creek Trailhead #2	N40.5793 W105.6185
3.2	Comanche Reservoir Dam and intersection with Hourglass Trail	N40.5855 W105.6449
4.1	Enter Comanche Peak Wilderness; end of Comanche Reservoir	N40.5872 W105.6610
4.7	Intersection with Comanche Lake Trail	N40.5902 W105.6697
4.7	Intersection with Browns Lake Trail	N40.5904 W105.6705
7.6	Cabin at intersection with Brackenbury Cabin Trail	N40.5938 W105.7142
7.7	Intersection with Flowers Trail	N40.5939 W105.7183

BEAVER CREEK TRAIL /
HOURGLASS TRAIL / COMANCHE LAKE TRAIL

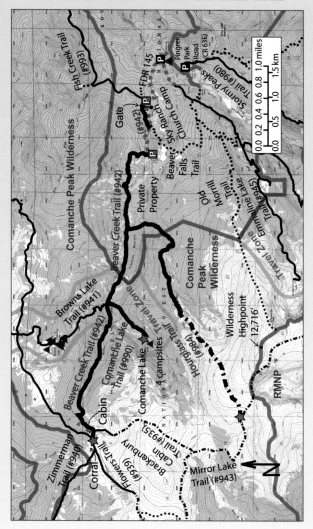

Hourglass Trail (#984)

TRAIL LENGTH	4.9 miles
TRAIL ELEVATION GAIN, LOSS, RANGE	2,656 feet, 421 feet, 9,370–11,963 feet
HIKE LENGTH	7.0 miles
HIKE ELEVATION GAIN, LOSS, RANGE	3,147 feet, 783 feet, 9,333–11,963 feet
DIFFICULTY RATING	Difficult; 11 percent average grade
STOCK RATING	Difficult
DOGS	Permitted on handheld leash
SEASON	Mid-June through late October; road to the trailhead closed due to snow in the off-season
TRAILS ILLUSTRATED MAP	Poudre River/Cameron Pass (#112)
USGS 7.5-MINUTE QUADS	Comanche Peak and Pingree Park

COMMENT: This trail provides a variety of scenery, starting at Comanche Reservoir, following along a splashing creek, through the forest and onto the alpine tundra. Although it is one of the steeper of the trails in the Comanche Peak Wilderness, the extra workout is well worth it, as the views from on top are wonderful.

GETTING THERE: From Fort Collins, take US 287 north to the intersection with Colorado 14 at Ted's Place. Travel west on Colorado 14 for 26 miles to Pingree Park Road (County Road 63E). Turn left and go 15.4 miles to the turnoff to Tom Bennett Campground (Forest Development Road 145). Follow FDR 145 for 1.3 miles to the trailhead just before Sky Ranch Camp. If the gate at the ranch is open (which it is almost all summer), you can drive another 1.2 miles to the second trailhead, but be aware that they sometimes close the gate if no one is at the camp, particularly outside the summer months. The trail from the first trailhead works its way around the camp and then

A few wildflowers can still be found along the Hourglass Trail in late August.

rejoins FDR 145 to the second trailhead. From the second trailhead, follow the Beaver Creek Trail for 2.1 miles to the Comanche Reservoir dam.

TRAIL DESCRIPTION: This trail starts at the northern side of the Comanche Reservoir dam. Comanche Reservoir is a pretty lake when it's full (typically earlier in the season). The trail crosses the dam to the south and enters into cool forest, following an unnamed creek. The rushing, splashing water provides refreshing sound effects. After about 0.75 mile, the trail makes a moderately steep climb out of the valley bottom and begins to follow a ridgeline to the southwest. The higher you get, the thinner the forest becomes, until eventually the trail breaks above timberline. The trail becomes faint near timberline and above, and there are also a couple of unmarked faint spur trails to unofficial campsites to the north (it's easy to accidentally follow these spur trails when descending this

Friends Terri Gerard and Steve Martin descend toward timberline on the Hourglass Trail.

trail). The views above timberline are great; you can see Crown Point to the north, numerous smaller peaks to the east, and the broad flank of Comanche Peak to the south. You can also look down on little Comanche Lake to the north. In the summer, there are a lot of alpine wildflowers along the trail, so bring along your wildflower book. The trail continues to climb less and less steeply until it tops out on a shoulder of the mountain. From here it descends a little to the Mirror Lake Trail, marked only by a post. If you've made it this far, then you must take the short 0.4-mile detour on the Mirror Lake Trail to the Mirror Lake overlook. The view down into and across this cirque is one of the most spectacular in the Comanche Peak Wilderness.

HOURGLASS TRAIL

MILEAGE	DESTINATIONS	GPS WAYPOINTS
0.0	Hourglass Trail intersection with Beaver Creek Trail	N40.5855 W105.6449
0.3	South end of Comanche Reservoir dam	N40.5814 W105.6426
0.7	Enter Comanche Peak Wilderness	N40.5774 W105.6446
4.9	Intersection with Mirror Lake Trail	N40.5567 W105.7086

SEE TRAIL MAP ON PAGE 75

Water cascades down an unnamed creek along the Hourglass Trail.

Comanche Lake Trail (#990)

TRAIL LENGTH	1.1 miles
TRAIL ELEVATION GAIN, LOSS, RANGE	449 feet, 21 feet, 9,540–9,984 feet
HIKE LENGTH	4.6 miles
HIKE ELEVATION GAIN, LOSS, RANGE	1,240 feet, 607 feet, 9,335–9,984 feet
DIFFICULTY RATING	Moderate; 8 percent average grade
STOCK RATING	Moderate (stock not permitted overnight within Travel Zone)
DOGS	Permitted on handheld leash
SEASON	Mid-June through late October; trailhead closed due to snow in the off-season
TRAILS ILLUSTRATED MAP	Poudre River/Cameron Pass (#112)
USGS 7.5-MINUTE QUADS	Comanche Peak and Pingree Park

COMMENT: This short trail branches off of the Beaver Creek Trail and winds its way through dense, mature subalpine evergreen forest to picturesque Comanche Lake. This is a great place for hikers and fishermen seeking solitude. Four designated campsites are dispersed around the lake, which also makes this an ideal destination for backpackers.

GETTING THERE: From Fort Collins, take US 287 north to the intersection with Colorado 14 at Ted's Place. Travel west on Colorado 14 for 26 miles to Pingree Park Road (County Road 63E). Turn left and go 15.4 miles to the turnoff to Tom Bennett Campground (Forest Development Road 145). Follow FDR 145 for 1.3 miles to the trailhead just before Sky Ranch Camp. If the gate at the ranch is open (which it is almost all summer), you can drive another 1.2 miles to the second trailhead, but be aware that they sometimes close the gate if no one is at the camp, particularly outside the summer months. The trail from

Comanche Lake is the delightful destination at the end of the trail.

the first trailhead works its way around the camp and then rejoins FDR 145 to the second trailhead. From the second trailhead, follow the Beaver Creek Trail for 3.6 miles to the start of the Comanche Lake Trail.

TRAIL DESCRIPTION: After branching off from the Beaver Creek Trail, the Comanche Lake Trail crosses Beaver Creek, then climbs somewhat steeply out of the Beaver Creek valley before leveling off and reaching beautiful Comanche Lake at its end. The lake is small, but very picturesque, offering a great hiking destination. There are four campsites around the lake, but they were not well marked at the time we hiked this trail. If you're going to camp, keep looking until you find one, as it is illegal to create your own campsite within this USFS Travel

Zone. Or, possibly a better option is to camp nearby along the Beaver Creek Trail outside of the Travel Zone. Equestrian campers, in particular, must camp outside of the Travel Zone, as stock are not permitted within the Travel Zone overnight.

Looking down on Comanche Lake from the Hourglass Trail.

COMANCHE LAKE TRAIL		
MILEAGE	DESTINATIONS	GPS WAYPOINTS
	Comanche Lake Trail intersection with Beaver Creek Trail	N40.5902 W105.6697
0.1	Cross Beaver Creek	N40.5894 W105.6704
1.1	Comanche Lake	N40.5809 W105.6822

SEE TRAIL MAP ON PAGE 75

Browns Lake Trail (#941)

TRAIL LENGTH	5.9 miles
ELEVATION GAIN, LOSS, RANGE	1,124 feet, 2,044 feet, 9,560–11,400 feet
DIFFICULTY RATING	Difficult; 10 percent average grade
STOCK RATING	Moderate (stock not permitted overnight within USFS Travel Zone)
DOGS	Permitted on handheld leash within Wilderness
SEASON	Mid-June through late October; trailhead closed due to snow in the off-season
TRAILS ILLUSTRATED MAP	Poudre River/Cameron Pass (#112)
USGS 7.5-MINUTE QUADS	Comanche Peak and Kinikinik

COMMENT: Despite the long drive on gravel roads, this hike is a must-do. Its trailhead lies only 600 feet below timberline, so it provides quick access to the alpine tundra and its multitude of wildflowers. The climb up to Crown Point is a great hike all by itself, with a mix of shady forest and scattered small meadows along the way. Beyond Crown Point, it continues across the open tundra, with awesome views all around. Beautiful Browns and Timberline Lakes, nestled in a glacial cirque, are the final destination for most hikers; however, the trail does continue farther downhill, ending at the Beaver Creek Trail.

GETTING THERE: From Fort Collins, take US 287 north to the intersection with Colorado 14 at Ted's Place. Travel west on Colorado 14 for 26 miles to Pingree Park Road (County Road 63E). Turn left and travel 4.2 miles to Crown Point Road (Forest Development Road 139). Turn right and travel 11.7 miles to the trailhead. At the trailhead there is a large gravel parking area on the right side of the road, while the trail and trail information is on the opposite side of the road.

Fog rolls in from the east toward Crown Point.

TRAIL DESCRIPTION: The trail starts with a short, steep climb through open limber pine forest, although it soon levels off. The ground is gravelly for a stretch, where the trail can be hard to follow; fortunately, volunteers have blocked most wrong turns with logs. As it nears timberline, the trail becomes steep again, and climbs onto the alpine tundra. The trail crests along a rocky ridgeline just to the west of Crown Point, where it enters the Comanche Peak Wilderness and a USFS Travel Zone. Stock animals are allowed to pass through this Travel Zone, but are not allowed to spend the night. The trail heads to the south from Crown Point down through a broad valley and up

the next ridge. The top of this ridge provides a stunning view of Comanche Peak to the south, as well as the rocky cirque surrounding Browns Lake to the southwest. From here, the trail descends back down through timberline, intersecting the Flowers Trail in a small meadow with an old cabin and a stream. Two Travel Zone designated campsites are located a short distance along the Flowers Trail, one in either direction. Between here and Browns and Timberline Lakes, there are ten more scattered backcountry campsites along the trail. Since this is a Travel Zone, you will need to bring a camp stove for all your cooking needs and you may only camp in designated

Browns Lake.

sites. This area is relatively popular for camping, so many sites
will be occupied on busy weekends. Before reaching the lakes,
the forest opens up, providing beautiful views of Browns Lake
below. The trail then descends down to the lake, where you will
typically find fishermen trying their luck in the summer. You
will also notice designated and nondesignated campsites
around the lake; if the designated sites (marked by a post with
a campsite number) are all taken, avoid the temptation to use
the nondesignated ones. Rangers frequently have to restore
these illegal sites to avoid further use. Rather, find a place just
outside of the Travel Zone and camp there. The trail wraps
around the east side of the lake and crosses a log bridge
between Browns and Timberline Lakes. After this point, the
trail becomes much fainter as it drops down toward Beaver
Creek through dense mature forest. Before the steep final
descent into the valley, it enters into a burn area where
there is a nice rock outcrop off to the side, providing pleasant
views down into the valley, including Comanche Reservoir
to the southeast.

NEARBY OFF-TRAIL DESTINATION

CROWN POINT (1.8 miles, 998 feet elevation gain+loss): Hike up the Browns Lake Trail to the Wilderness boundary. From here, follow the ridgeline uphill 0.1 mile to the nearest of three rock outcrops on the broad summit (N40.6293 W105.6843), making sure to minimize your impact on the alpine tundra. The summit provides magnificent views of the surrounding mountain ranges, particularly the Medicine Bow Range to the west and the Mummy Range with massive Comanche Peak to the south.

BROWNS LAKE TRAIL		
MILEAGE	DESTINATIONS	GPS WAYPOINTS
	Browns Lake Trailhead	N40.6497 W105.6985
1.7	Enter Wilderness and Travel Zone just below Crown Point	N40.6295 W105.6869
3.1	Intersection with Flowers Trail	N40.6131 W105.6813
4.3	Browns Lake	N40.6035 W105.6845
4.4	Timberline Lake	N40.6029 W105.6842
5.1	Overlook	N40.5967 W105.6748
5.9	Intersection with Beaver Creek Trail	N40.5904 W105.6705

CAMPSITES

Campsite #1	N40.6126 W105.6828
Campsite #2	N40.6137 W105.6803
Campsite #3	N40.6103 W105.6799
Campsite #4	N40.6088 W105.6800
Campsite #5	N40.6065 W105.6838
Campsite #6	N40.6044 W105.6837
Campsite #7	N40.6044 W105.6837
Campsite #8	N40.6020 W105.6836
Campsite #9	N40.6017 W105.6827
Campsite #10	N40.6059 W105.6864
Campsite #11	N40.6024 W105.6848
Campsite #12	N40.6024 W105.6841

BROWNS LAKE TRAIL

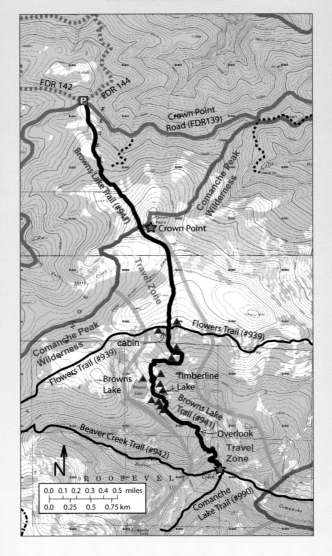

Zimmerman Trail (#940)

TRAIL LENGTH	6.3 miles
ELEVATION GAIN, LOSS, RANGE	279 feet, 2,015 feet, 9,450–11,164 feet
DIFFICULTY RATING	Moderate; 7 percent average grade
STOCK RATING	Moderate
DOGS	Permitted on handheld leash within Wilderness
SEASON	Mid-June through late October; trailhead closed due to snow in the off-season
TRAILS ILLUSTRATED MAP	Poudre River/Cameron Pass (#112)
USGS 7.5-MINUTE QUADS	Boston Peak, Chambers Lake, Comanche Peak, and Kinikinik

COMMENT: Unique among the trailheads in this guide, the Zimmerman Trailhead is located in the middle of the trail. It is the highest trailhead of any in the Comanche Peak Wilderness. The southern section of the trail provides quick access to open expanses of tundra, and to four other trails. The northern section, on the other hand, winds through shady forest before reaching the most beautiful meadow in this guide.

GETTING THERE: From Fort Collins, take US 287 north to the intersection with Colorado 14 at Ted's Place. Travel west on Colorado 14 for 26 miles to Pingree Park Road (County Road 63E). Turn left and travel 4.2 miles to Crown Point Road (Forest Development Road 139). Turn right and travel 18.2 miles to the end of the road, where you'll find the Zimmerman Trailhead.

TRAIL DESCRIPTION:

SOUTHERN SECTION: This section of the trail starts by heading gently uphill to the south through dense spruce forest, with a carpet of kinnikinnick and grouseberry below. After about 1 mile, the grade starts to level off and the forest begins to

Beautiful Sheep Creek Meadow lies along the Zimmerman Trail.

open up, as the trail follows a ridge just below timberline. Along this portion, the trail can be somewhat hard to follow for short sections, so rock cairns have been placed to mark the way. The trail meanders for a little more than 1 mile, allowing occasional glimpses of the alpine slopes above. Eventually it climbs up above treeline, where it meets the Flowers Trail on an alpine meadow. From this point, you have many options for continuing your hike, as nearby intersections provide access to four other trails (see map).

NORTHERN SECTION: This section of the trail starts by gradually descending toward the north through somewhat open forest. You can catch a few small glimpses of the Medicine Bow Range through the trees to the northwest, but other than that, it's pretty much a tree tunnel. After about 2.5 miles, the trail starts to make a steep descent into the West Fork of the Sheep Creek valley. At the valley bottom, it starts to level out and crosses a small unnamed creek (there is no bridge). Shortly thereafter, you will come upon the large and beautiful Sheep Creek Meadow, where the East and West Forks of Sheep Creek slowly wind their way across the meadow before converging at the north end. This is, in our opinion, the most beautiful meadow along any Comanche Peak Wilderness trail, although it actually lies just outside of the Wilderness boundary. Moose frequent the area, as there is plenty of water and willows. Hardy fishermen also like to try to catch greenback trout here. Bring strong mosquito repellent, because the mosquitoes here are usually ferocious. The trail becomes faint to nonexistent as it works its way along the west side of the meadow. The maintained portion of the trail ends at the far northwestern

A view to the north as the Zimmerman Trail breaks above timberline.

corner of the meadow, where the trail crosses Sheep Creek. We were able to cross the wide and fast-flowing creek on a log jam, but there is no guarantee that it will remain there. Since the trail is no longer maintained past the Sheep Creek crossing, the final portion of the trail is not included in the trail statistics. However, those who wish to continue north on this trail can still enjoy a nice hike through the forest. This section follows along the remnants of a dam for what used to be Sheep Creek Reservoir. A portion of the dam blocks what was the East Fork, creating a splendid wetland for waterfowl and fish. At the far end of the dam are the rotting remnants of three log cabins. From here, the trail follows an old roadbed up to an intersection with the Sheep Creek Cutoff Trail. The Sheep Creek Cutoff Trailhead lies along FDR 142, which can only be accessed by high-clearance vehicles. Beyond this intersection, the trail becomes substantially fainter, nearly nonexistent in spots. Occasional blazes on the trees help to lead the way. After a short distance, the trail tops out and begins a long and sometimes steep descent into an unnamed valley, eventually ending in the Cache la Poudre Canyon. Because of its extensive length, the abundance of downfall, and the fact that it ends at private property, rarely does anyone hike to its end.

ZIMMERMAN TRAIL		
MILEAGE	**DESTINATIONS**	**GPS WAYPOINTS**
2.6	Intersection with Flowers Trail	N40.5932 W105.7210
0.0	Zimmerman Trailhead	N40.6099 W105.7565
2.9	Leave Wilderness	N40.6448 W105.7532
3.1	Reach Sheep Creek Meadow	N40.6474 W105.7521
3.7	Sheep Creek crossing (end of maintained trail)	N40.6552 W105.7485
3.9	Old cabins	N40.6555 W105.7454
4.7	Intersection with Sheep Creek Cutoff Trail	N40.6618 W105.7386
9.1	End of trail at private property boundary	N40.6928 W105.6887

ZIMMERMAN TRAIL

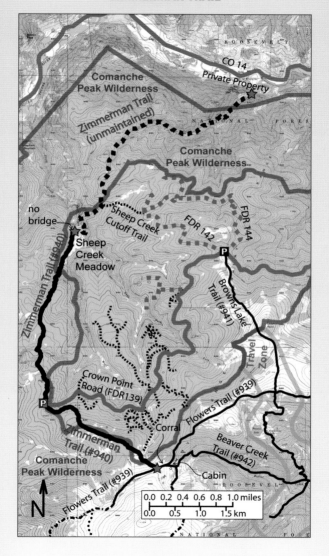

COMANCHE PEAK WILDERNESS AREA—CROWN POINT SECTION

Brackenbury Cabin
Trail (#935, formerly #1010)

TRAIL LENGTH	2.1 miles
TRAIL ELEVATION GAIN, LOSS, RANGE	728 feet, 492 feet, 10,957–11,631 feet
HIKE LENGTH	5.0 miles
HIKE ELEVATION GAIN, LOSS, RANGE	1,450 feet, 873 feet, 10,616–11,631 feet
DIFFICULTY RATING	Moderate; 10 percent average grade
STOCK RATING	Easy
DOGS	Permitted on handheld leash
SEASON	Mid-June through late October; trailhead closed due to snow in the off-season
TRAILS ILLUSTRATED MAP	Poudre River/Cameron Pass (#112)
USGS 7.5-MINUTE QUAD	Comanche Peak

COMMENT: This short trail is a good one if you love alpine wildflowers, as it climbs over a broad alpine pass. For those wanting a more serious hike, it can be used as a shortcut over to the Mirror Lake Trail. Along the way, there are broad beautiful views to the north, east, and south; and, of course, you get to see the remnants of the old Brackenbury Cabin.

GETTING THERE: From Fort Collins, take US 287 north to the intersection with Colorado 14 at Ted's Place. Travel west on Colorado 14 for 26 miles to Pingree Park Road (County Road 63E). Turn left and go 4.2 miles to Crown Point Road (Forest Development Road 139). Turn right and travel 18.2 miles to the end of the road, where you'll find the Zimmerman Trailhead. Follow the southern section of the Zimmerman Trail for 2.6 miles to the intersection with the Flowers Trail. Turn left and hike 0.1 mile to the intersection with the Beaver

There is a nice view of the Never Summer Range at the intersection of the Brackenbury Cabin and Mirror Lake Trails, marked by a broken sign in a cairn.

Creek Trail. Turn right and hike 0.2 mile downhill to the start of the Brackenbury Cabin Trail.

TRAIL DESCRIPTION: The Brackenbury Cabin Trail starts from the Beaver Creek Trail near the remnants of the old Brackenbury sheepherder's cabin. It heads south and shortly crosses over Beaver Creek; rocks in the creek provide stepping stones to get across. From here, it begins a steady climb to the south up to an unnamed saddle. The trail becomes faint to nonexistent on the climb, but occasional 1- to 3-foot-high rock

Frédérique and our puppy Poudre hiking across the gently rolling slopes on the Brackenbury Cabin Trail.

cairns mark the way. As you get higher, broad sweeping views open up to the west. But don't just look at the views; look down at your feet to a natural garden of wildflowers in the summer. One time while hiking this trail we stopped and counted fifteen different species around us. The climb becomes more and more gradual as you near the pass. As you crest it, you'll be amazed at the new views that greet you to the south of numerous majestic peaks in the Mummy and Never Summer Ranges. The trail then descends down to its intersection with the Mirror Lake Trail near timberline.

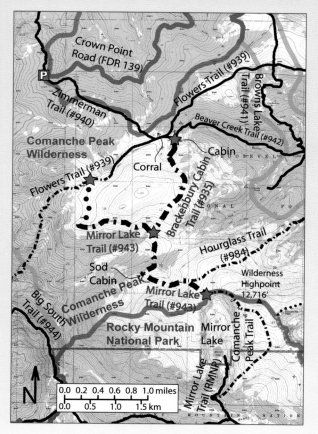

BRACKENBURY CABIN TRAIL

MILEAGE	DESTINATIONS	GPS WAYPOINTS
	Remains of Brackenbury Cabin at intersection with Beaver Creek Trail	N40.5938 W105.7142
1.4	Pass	N40.5767 W105.7141
2.1	Intersection with Mirror Lake Trail	N40.5687 W105.7209

Mirror Lake Trail (#943)

TRAIL LENGTH	4.5 miles
TRAIL ELEVATION GAIN, LOSS, RANGE	1,387 feet, 621 feet, 11,004–12,017 feet
HIKE LENGTH	8.6 miles
HIKE ELEVATION GAIN, LOSS, RANGE	2,399 feet, 1,018 feet, 10,616–12,017 feet
DIFFICULTY RATING	Moderate; 8 percent average grade
STOCK RATING	Moderate
DOGS	Permitted on handheld leash
SEASON	Mid-June through late October; trailhead closed due to snow in the off-season
TRAILS ILLUSTRATED MAP	Poudre River/Cameron Pass (#112)
USGS 7.5-MINUTE QUAD	Comanche Peak

COMMENT: The highest trail in the Comanche Peak Wilderness, the Mirror Lake Trail provides a variety of alpine views. And since it is so remote, the trail is faint to nonexistent in places, so you are likely to have it all to yourself. The highlights of this trail are the sod cabin and the magnificent Mirror Lake overlook. This also is a good trail for appreciating wildflowers in the summer.

GETTING THERE: From Fort Collins, take US 287 north to the intersection with Colorado 14 at Ted's Place. Travel west on Colorado 14 for 26 miles to Pingree Park Road (County Road 63E). Turn left and go 4.2 miles to Crown Point Road (Forest Development Road 139). Turn right and travel 18.2 miles to the end of the road, where you'll find the Zimmerman Trailhead. Follow the southern section of the Zimmerman Trail for 2.6 miles to the intersection with the Flowers Trail. Turn right and hike another 1.5 miles to the start of the Mirror Lake Trail.

An old sod cabin sits near timberline along the Mirror Lake Trail.

TRAIL DESCRIPTION: Don't confuse this trail with the trail of the same name in Rocky Mountain National Park. This trail ends at an overlook of Mirror Lake, while the one in the National Park actually takes you to the lake itself. This trail starts along the Flowers Trail at a small alpine saddle. However, there is no visible indication of a trail at the intersection, only a line on the map. This saddle provides awesome views in all directions, including the impressive sight of the Never Summer Range to the west and southwest, and the Medicine Bow Range to the northwest. The route heads south from here through widely scattered stunted trees, generally holding an elevation of 11,280 feet. There are plenty

The Mirror Lake Trail ends with this amazing view down into and across the Mirror Lake cirque, fringed by permanent snow fields.

of wildflowers in the summer. As it rounds a ridge with a few small rock outcrops, you will come upon a rock cairn; from here on, occasional 1- to 3-foot-tall cairns mark the trail, although there is little to no visible indication of a path. Along this stretch of the trail, you have a nice view across the Willow Creek valley to two broad unnamed peaks to the south. At the intersection with the Brackenbury Cabin Trail (marked by a post in a rock cairn), the trail turns south and drops down into the Willow Creek valley. This valley is aptly named; dense willows line its bottom, with the trail providing the only easy access across. Just before reaching the creek, you'll enter into a little piece of forest. Backpackers and hunters have made their camps here in the past, so the already faint trail splits here into several even fainter trails. Please respect Wilderness regulations and do not camp within 200 feet of the trail or the creek, even though others have. Better yet, please camp out of sight of the trail. We want this area to return to its natural state. If you are able to find the trail, follow it across the creek and up the steep bank on the other side. If you lose it, just climb the opposite bank and look for the line of cairns that work their way southwest, hugging timberline. This southwest jaunt seems contradictory to where the trail is supposed to lead to the southeast, but is well worth the detour, as it leads to a small sod cabin, the best preserved cabin we know of in the Comanche Peak Wilderness. The roof leaks, but you can still see an old stove, table, and shelves inside. From here, the trail leaves the shelter of timberline and follows small cairns gently uphill to the southeast toward the Mirror Lake overlook. Along the way, it intersects the Hourglass Trail, marked only by a post. Eventually, it tops out at the Mirror Lake overlook, which is also the boundary with the National Park. The views from here are stupendous, as Mirror Lake and another unnamed lake lie at the base of this steep-walled cirque. In the distance, you can also see the three highest peaks in the Mummy Range: Hagues Peak, Fairchild Mountain, and Ypsilon Mountain, as well as several smaller peaks. Although there is not a sign to indicate it, the trail changes names here to the Comanche Peak Trail. Cairns do not mark this section of trail; rather, it follows posts along the Park boundary. If you want, you can follow this trail around and down to Mirror Lake itself. Or, you can make your way over to the nearby 12,716-foot Comanche Peak Wilderness highpoint.

MIRROR LAKE TRAIL		
MILEAGE	**DESTINATIONS**	**GPS WAYPOINTS**
0.0	Mirror Lake Trail intersection with Flowers Trail (undefined)	N40.5823 W105.7421
2.3	Intersection with Brackenbury Cabin Trail	N40.5687 W105.7209
3.2	Sod cabin	N40.5582 W105.7236
4.1	Intersection with Hourglass Trail	N40.5567 W105.7086
4.5	Mirror Lake overlook	N40.5530 W105.7011

SEE TRAIL MAP ON PAGE 97

Sleeping Elephant Mountain

(off-trail destination)

HIKE LENGTH	1.1 miles
HIKE ELEVATION GAIN, LOSS, RANGE	1,301 feet, 11 feet, 7,855–9,145 feet
DIFFICULTY RATING	Difficult; 23 percent average grade
STOCK RATING	Not recommended
DOGS	Permitted on handheld leash within Wilderness
SEASON	Early September through late October; the route is accessible year-round, but a river crossing makes it very difficult in spring and summer, and deep snow makes for a very difficult ascent in winter
TRAILS ILLUSTRATED MAP	Poudre River/Cameron Pass (#112)
USGS 7.5-MINUTE QUAD	Boston Peak

COMMENT: Sleeping Elephant Mountain, arguably the most recognizable peak in the Comanche Peak Wilderness, lies along its northwestern boundary. At 9,145 feet, it is also the lowest of the named peaks in the Wilderness. There is no established trail to this peak.

GETTING THERE: From Fort Collins, take US 287 north to the intersection with Colorado 14 at Ted's Place. Travel west on Colorado 14 for about 44 miles, about 0.3 mile short of the Colorado Department of Transportation station in Spencer Heights. There's no official trailhead or parking area for this hike, so you'll need to find a pull-off along the highway that isn't on private property. We used a small pull-off near the Sleeping Elephant Campground (N40.6821 W105.7733).

It is obvious how Sleeping Elephant Mountain got its name.

ROUTE DESCRIPTION: From the road, look at the mountainside and identify the route drawn in red on the photo on the following page. This route passes above a major diagonal cliff band and then switchbacks through a weakness in a minor cliff band. There is no longer a bridge that crosses the river here, so you will need to wade the river. This is best done in the late summer or fall, after the river level has dropped and before a deep coat of snow has covered the mountain. Crossing the river during high runoff can be dangerous. After crossing it, make your way across a long, pretty meadow, being sure to go around the corner of private property (N40.6782 W105.7748); the boundary is marked by occasional National Forest boundary signs. Once at the base of the mountain, head very steeply up the mountain and follow one of the many game trails that lead up the slope; eventually almost all of them converge onto a single well-worn game trail (N40.6766 W105.7720) that will take you past the two sets of cliff bands.

A view of Sleeping Elephant Mountain from Highway 14, with the easiest route to the summit marked in red.

As you near the top, the slope begins to lessen and the trail disappears, but continue to work your way diagonally up the slope to the left until you are due south of the summit. Then head north to the top of the ridge and follow it to the summit. The true summit is located on the "shoulders" of the elephant (N40.6774 W105.7660) and provides a wonderful view in every direction. A short jaunt over to the "head" (N40.6780 W105.7651) provides the best vertical view down into the valley below.

Looking up the Cache la Poudre River valley from the top of a rock band on the route up Sleeping Elephant Mountain.

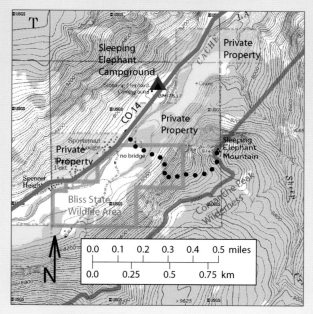

Have you enjoyed this challenging off-trail hike?

Would you like to find out about other hikes to impressive, yet unnamed peaks and lakes that weren't able to make it into this book? Would you like to see very detailed maps, trail profiles, and hundreds of photos that weren't able to make it into the book? Then go to the Comanche Peak Wilderness Web site at **www.joeandfrede.com/comanche.htm**. Over the next several years, we plan to continue to add new hikes, new photos, and much more.

Big South Trail (#944)

TRAIL LENGTH	10.5 miles
ELEVATION GAIN, LOSS, RANGE	1,811 feet, 713 feet, 8,438–9,704 feet
DIFFICULTY RATING	Moderate; 5 percent average grade
STOCK RATING	Not recommended on lower (northern) section; moderate on upper section
DOGS	Permitted on handheld leash within Wilderness
SEASON	Trailhead accessible year-round; snowshoes typically necessary November–May
TRAILS ILLUSTRATED MAP	Poudre River/Cameron Pass (#112)
USGS 7.5-MINUTE QUADS	Boston Peak, Chambers Lake, and Comanche Peak

COMMENT: This trail follows along a wild upper stretch of the Cache la Poudre River for its entire 10-plus-mile length, providing great hiking, fishing, and backcountry camping. You won't have broad, sweeping views along this trail, but the cool shade of the forest and the rushing water of the Cache la Poudre River make this a very pleasant summer hike. This trail is accessible all year round, although the canyon narrows a couple miles up the trail, which makes the trail hard to find in the winter.

GETTING THERE:

BIG SOUTH TRAILHEAD: From Fort Collins, take US 287 north to the intersection with Colorado 14 at Ted's Place. Travel west on Colorado 14 for 48 miles to the trailhead, which is on the left side of the highway.

PETERSON LAKE TRAILHEAD: Follow the directions for the Big South Trailhead, then continue west on Colorado 14 for another 6 miles to Long Draw Road. Turn left and follow the road for 3.5 miles to Peterson Lake Road. Veer left onto this

The Big South Trail parallels the Cache la Poudre River for its entire length.

road and go 1.8 miles to Peterson Lake. Find a place to pull off the road here unless you have a four-wheel-drive high-clearance vehicle, in which case you can continue another 0.3 mile to the Peterson Lake Trailhead. From the trailhead, follow the Peterson Lake Trail to the southwest for 0.8 mile to its intersection with the Big South Trail.

CORRAL CREEK TRAILHEAD: See Corral Creek Trail description.

TRAIL DESCRIPTION: This trail has two sections, separated by a washed-out bridge.

LOWER SECTION: The lower section of Big South Trail extends for the first 7.0 miles of the 10.5-mile trail. The entire trail travels up the narrow Cache la Poudre Canyon, and therefore it

A calm section of the Cache la Poudre River.

is necessary for the trail to go through a series of ups and downs in order to find the best path, making what would otherwise be an easy hike into a moderate one. The trail is rather rocky in places, and as a result, stock are not recommended on the lower section of the trail; however, stock are fine on the upper section of the trail. After hiking 0.5 mile from the trailhead, you'll enter the Comanche Peak Wilderness and the Big South Travel Zone, where Wilderness and Travel Zone rules apply. Within the Travel Zone, the trail passes near sixteen designated campsites, each of which can be found at the end of short spur trails marked by numbered signs. Since this is a Travel Zone, any backpackers need to remember to bring their camp stoves for cooking, as campfires are not allowed. After campsite 9, the trail starts to level out and becomes an easy stroll through the forest. Eventually, it intersects the Flowers Trail just below where a bridge used to span the river. If you want to hike the southern (upper) portion of the Big South Trail, it's usually best not to wade the river, except in late summer or fall; instead, you can reach that portion of the trail from either the Peterson Lake or Corral Creek Trailheads.

UPPER SECTION: Since most people hike the upper portion of the trail from the Corral Creek Trailhead (see Corral Creek Trail description), the description for this part of the trail will start from the east end of the Corral Creek Trail. The trail starts by passing through a few small, flat meadows before entering into the forest. The drop of the river increases, creating a series of rapids and cascades interspersed with some calmer stretches. Along this stretch you'll pass by four designated backcountry campsites (numbered 17–20). Campsite 18, in our opinion, has the best location of any site, because it is so close to the best stretch of river along the trail. You'll sometimes see kayakers shooting the rapids in mid-summer. Farther downstream, the river becomes calmer again. A short distance after passing the remnants of two small cabins, the trail begins to climb somewhat steeply to the south out of the river bottom, in order to avoid a very narrow and steep portion of the canyon. It makes its way over a minor pass and begins to descend back toward the river. The intersection with the Peterson Lake Trail is shortly after the descent begins, and a short distance farther you'll pass by another old cabin. The final descent down to the river is steep, and you'll encounter several side trails used by fishermen. Eventually, it will become difficult to determine which trail is the real trail. This is a good place to turn around, unless the water level is low and you want to risk crossing the river to continue on the trail on the other side.

BIG SOUTH TRAIL

MILEAGE	DESTINATIONS	GPS WAYPOINTS
	Big South Trailhead	N40.6344 W105.8072
0.5	Enter Comanche Peak Wilderness	N40.6287 W105.8046
1.3	Campsite #1	N40.6204 W105.7994
1.3	Campsite #2	N40.6193 W105.7995
1.5	Campsite #3	N40.6162 W105.7988
1.5	Campsite #4	N40.6156 W105.7993
1.7	Campsite #5	N40.6131 W105.8000
2.4	Campsite #6	N40.6076 W105.7951
2.4	Bridge across May Creek	N40.6073 W105.7955
2.6	Campsite #7	N40.6048 W105.7944
3.3	Campsite #8	N40.5960 W105.8004
3.4	Campsite #9	N40.5960 W105.8011
4.9	Campsite #10	N40.5781 W105.8029
5.5	Campsite #11	N40.5710 W105.7955
5.6	Campsite #12	N40.5698 W105.7949
5.7	Campsite #13	N40.5681 W105.7938
5.9	Campsite #14	N40.5671 W105.7926
6.2	Campsite #15	N40.5635 W105.7885
6.3	Campsite #16	N40.5622 W105.7872
6.8	Flowers Trail intersection	N40.5567 W105.7788
7.0	Trail crosses river (no bridge)	N40.5562 W105.7784
7.5	Old cabin	N40.5502 W105.7757
7.6	Intersection with Peterson Lake Trail	N40.5492 W105.7756
8.4	Two old cabins	N40.5473 W105.7632
8.7	Campsite #17	N40.5435 W105.7599
9.4	Campsite #18	N40.5368 W105.7548
9.7	Campsite #19	N40.5334 W105.7533
9.8	Campsite #20	N40.5323 W105.7533
10.5	Intersection with Corral Creek and Poudre River Trails	N40.5235 W105.7498

NOTE: The GPS waypoints for each campsite listed above are for the site itself and not for the start of the spur trail to the site, as these trails are sometimes quite faint and hard to follow; however, signs mark the start of most campsite spur trails.

BIG SOUTH TRAIL / CORRAL CREEK TRAIL

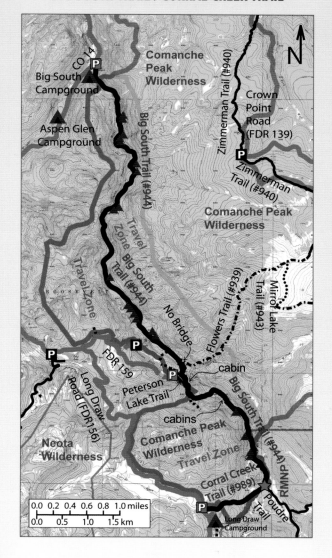

Corral Creek Trail (#989)

TRAIL LENGTH	1.3 miles
ELEVATION GAIN, LOSS, RANGE	0 feet; 363 feet; 9,675–10,038 feet
DIFFICULTY RATING	Easy; 5 percent average grade
STOCK RATING	Easy
DOGS	Permitted on handheld leash within Wilderness; not permitted to enter National Park
SEASON	Early July through late October; trailhead closed due to snow in the off-season
TRAILS ILLUSTRATED MAP	Poudre River/Cameron Pass (#112)
USGS 7.5-MINUTE QUADS	Chambers Lake and Comanche Peak

COMMENT: This short trail follows Corral Creek, passing through forest and meadows, and is great for those seeking a short, easy hike, or for fishermen hoping to try their luck on Poudre Pass Creek or the Cache la Poudre River. It's also a great jumping-off point for those seeking to explore the remote northwestern corner of Rocky Mountain National Park and the upper stretches of the Big South Trail.

GETTING THERE: From Fort Collins, take US 287 north to the intersection with Colorado 14 at Ted's Place. Travel west on Colorado 14 for 54 miles to Long Draw Road (Forest Development Road 156). Turn left and follow the road for 8.5 miles to the trailhead, which is on the left side of the road

TRAIL DESCRIPTION: The trail follows Corral Creek for its entire length, passing through forest and flowery meadows. It ends at an intersection with the Big South and Poudre River Trails. This trail is often used by anglers and kayakers to access the Cache la Poudre River, as well as by hikers who want to access the trails of the remote northwestern section of

A bridge crosses over Poudre Pass Creek near the three-way intersection of the Corral Creek, Big South, and Poudre River Trails.

Low clouds hung over a meadow as we hiked down the Corral Creek Trail.

Rocky Mountain National Park. It enters into the Comanche Peak Wilderness shortly after the trailhead, so Wilderness rules apply.

Morning mist rises up from the forest.

CORRAL CREEK TRAIL		
MILEAGE	**DESTINATIONS**	**GPS WAYPOINTS**
	Corral Creek Trailhead	N40.5179 W105.7703
1.3	Intersection with Big South and Poudre River Trails	N40.5235 W105.7498

SEE TRAIL MAP ON PAGE 111

TRAIL INFORMATION

TRAIL RANKING

BY DISTANCE		BY HIGHEST ELEVATION	
Trail or Hike Name	**Distance[1]**	**Trail or Hike Name**	**Highest Elevation[2]**
Corral Creek Trail	1.3	Fish Creek Trail	9,186
Comanche Lake Trail	4.6	North Fork Trail	9,278
Brackenbury Cabin Trail	5.0	Big South Trail	9,704
Stormy Peaks Trail	5.2	*North Boundary Trail*	9,710
North Fork Trail	5.3	Little Beaver Creek Trail	9,797
Bulwark Ridge Trail	5.4	*Comanche Lake Trail*	9,984
Emmaline Lake Trail	5.9	Corral Creek Trail	10,038
Browns Lake Trail	5.9	Emmaline Lake Trail	11,015
Signal Mountain Trail	6.0	*Bulwark Ridge Trail*	11,042
North Boundary Trail	6.1	Beaver Creek Trail	11,128
Zimmerman Trail	6.1	Zimmerman Trail	11,164
Fish Creek Trail	6.4	Signal Mountain Trail	11,200
Hourglass Trail	7.0	Flowers Trail	11,318
Little Beaver Creek Trail	7.1	Browns Lake Trail	11,400
Mummy Pass Trail	7.2	*Mummy Pass Trail*	11,461
Beaver Creek Trail	7.7	*Brackenbury Cabin Trail*	11,631
Mirror Lake Trail	8.6	Stormy Peaks Trail	11,667
Big South Trail	10.5	*Hourglass Trail*	11,963
Flowers Trail	15.0	*Mirror Lake Trail*	12,017

[1] **Distance is one-way in miles from nearest trailhead**

[2] **Elevation in feet**

Trail names in italics indicate trails that require hiking on other trails to reach them; the information is for the total hike.

TRAIL RANKING

BY STEEPNESS		BY ELEVATION CHANGE	
Trail or Hike Name	Average Grade[3]	Trail or Hike Name	Total Gain+Loss[4]
Big South Trail	5	Corral Creek Trail	363
Corral Creek Trail	5	*Comanche Lake Trail*	1,847
Little Beaver Creek Trail	6	Fish Creek Trail	2,060
Fish Creek Trail	6	North Fork Trail	2,108
Zimmerman Trail	7	Emmaline Lake Trail	2,178
Emmaline Lake Trail	7	Little Beaver Creek Trail	2,211
Comanche Lake Trail	8	Zimmerman Trail	2,294
Beaver Creek Trail	8	*Brackenbury Cabin Trail*	2,323
Mummy Pass Trail	8	Big South Trail	2,524
Mirror Lake Trail	8	Stormy Peaks Trail	2,703
Flowers Trail	8	Signal Mountain Trail	3,104
North Fork Trail	8	*Mummy Pass Trail*	3,113
Brackenbury Cabin Trail	10	Browns Lake Trail	3,168
Signal Mountain Trail	10	Beaver Creek Trail	3,306
Browns Lake Trail	10	*Mirror Lake Trail*	3,417
Stormy Peaks Trail	10	*Bulwark Ridge Trail*	3,511
Hourglass Trail	11	North Boundary Trail	3,885
Bulwark Ridge Trail	12	*Hourglass Trail*	3,930
North Boundary Trail	12	Flowers Trail	6,283

[3] Grade given in percent for entire hike

[4] Elevation Gain+Loss = total gain round-trip

Trail names in italics indicate trails that require hiking on other trails to reach them; the information is for the total hike.

DISTANCE TO TRAILHEAD

IN MILES FROM
1. US 287 AND US 34 (LOVELAND)
2. US 287 AND CO 14 (TED'S PLACE)

Trail or Hike Name	Distance	From
Dunraven Trailhead North Fork Trail *Bulwark Ridge Trail*	25	1
Cow Creek Trailhead *North Boundary Trail*	30	1
Jack's Gulch Trailhead Little Beaver Creek	33	2
Fish Creek Trailhead Fish Creek Trail	34	2
Flowers Trailhead	36	2
Signal Mountain Trailhead	39	2
Emmaline Lake Trailhead Emmaline Lake Trail *Mummy Pass Trail*	42	2
Browns Lake Trailhead	42	2
Stormy Peaks Trailhead	42	2
Beaver Creek Trailhead Beaver Creek Trail *Hourglass Trail* *Comanche Lake Trail* Fish Creek Trail	43	2
Big South Trailhead	48	2
Zimmerman Trailhead Zimmerman Trail *Brackenbury Trail* *Mirror Lake Trail*	49	2
Peterson Lake Trailhead Big South Trail	58	2
Corral Creek Trailhead	62	2

GETTING INVOLVED

Have you enjoyed the beautiful Comanche Peak Wilderness? Would you like to be involved in making sure that it remains such a wonderful place for years and years to come? Wilderness and other backcountry areas, and especially the trails that pass through them, require regular oversight and maintenance. Tasks include maintaining trails and bridges; educating others about Leave No Trace principles and other land stewardship topics; documenting the presence and abundance of wildlife and plant species; monitoring the use levels and status of campgrounds, trails, and campsites; and many other service opportunities. Much of this work is accomplished by permanent and seasonal employees of government agencies such as the US Forest Service. However, with the increasing numbers of people each year who visit great areas such as this one, governmental funds and personnel numbers are falling well short of the ever-increasing number needed for this work, so public involvement is needed.

Volunteers are stepping up to address these unmet steward-ship needs. If you enjoy the outdoors, we encourage you to volunteer some of your time to give back to the natural resources and environments that have provided so much pleasure, enjoyment, and relaxation to you and others. Volunteer opportunities abound, both with government agencies and through public nonprofit organizations. Below are just a few of the many local organizations that welcome volunteers:

POUDRE WILDERNESS VOLUNTEERS—volunteer ranger program for the Canyon Lakes Ranger District of the Arapaho and Roosevelt National Forests (www.poudrewildernessvolunteers.org)

Other volunteer programs for the **CANYON LAKES RANGER DISTRICT** of the Arapaho and Roosevelt National Forests (www.fs.fed.us/r2/arnf/volunteering/projects-and-programs/clrdprojectsandprograms.shtml)

Wildflowers now abound along the Emmaline Lake Trail where the 1994 Hourglass Fire occurred.

LARIMER COUNTY NATURAL RESOURCES volunteer program
(www.co.larimer.co.us/naturalresources/volunteer/)

CITY OF FORT COLLINS NATURAL AREAS volunteer programs
(www.fcgov.com/naturalareas/volunteers.php)

THE COLORADO MOUNTAIN CLUB (www.cmc.org)

Thanks to Jim Shaklee for his work on this section.

ABOUT THE AUTHORS
Joe and Frédérique Grim

PHOTO BY MANUEL FILLON

Joe and Frédérique Grim have been happily married for more than eleven years, and they spend as much time as they can out in the mountains. Joe has a doctorate in Atmospheric Sciences and is employed by the National Center for Atmospheric Research, and Frédérique has a doctorate in French Applied Linguistics and is a professor at Colorado State University. Both Joe and Frédérique are members of the Fort Collins chapter of The Colorado Mountain Club, and Joe is a trip leader. They have contributed to two other CMC Press books, *Hiking Colorado's Roadless Trails* (2007) and *The Best Fort Collins Hikes* (2008), as well as *Afoot and Afield: Denver/Boulder and Colorado's Front Range* (2008) from Wilderness Press.